Pruning

SMITH & HAWKEN

The Hands·On Gardener

Pruning

by ROBERT KOURIK

with illustrations

by JIM ANDERSON

WORKMAN PUBLISHING · NEW YORK

To my late grandparents, Henry and Blanche Kourik
and Roas Tevis, watching them clip flowers
inspired my fascination with pruning.

This book couldn't have been written without the generous assistance of: Barbara Barton, author; John Britton, Consulting Arborist; Lucy Bradley, University of Arizona Cooperative Extension; Martha Casselman, my agent; Thomas Christopher, rosarian and author; Ben Chu and Chip Tynan of the Missouri Botanical Garden; Barrie Coate, Aboricultural/Horticultural Consultant; Bonnie Dahan of Smith & Hawken; Barbara Damrosch, author; John Dunmire, former editor of the *Sunset Western Garden Book*; Bill Grant, rosarian; Carolyn Harrison, Sonoma Antique Apple Nursery; Mary Irish, of the Desert Botanical Garden; James MacNair, Consulting Arborist; Ed Mulrean, Arid Zone Trees; Robert Stebbins and Melvin Westwood, professors Emeriti, Oregon State University; and Maggie Wych, Western Hills Nursery. Thanks to Sally Kovalchick and John Meils of Workman Publishing. And for support: my Dad, John Kourik; Chester Aaron; Michael Eschenbach; Mimi Luebbermann; and Salli Rasberry.

Published simultaneously in Canada by Thomas Allen & Son Limited.

Library of Congress Cataloging-in-Publication Data
Kourik, Robert, 1957–
Pruning / by Robert Kourik; illustrations by Jim Anderson
p. cm.—(Smith & Hawken—the hands-on gardener)
Includes index.
ISBN 0-7611-0806-8
1. Pruning.
I. Anderson, Jim. II. Title III. Series.
SB125.K65 1997
635.9' 1542—dc21   97-8881
CIP

Workman Publishing Company
708 Broadway, New York, NY 10003-9555

Manufactured in the United States of America

First printing April 1997
10 9 8 7 6 5 4 3 2 1

CONTENTS

A Pruning Primer

Gardeners often have extreme reactions to the task of pruning; they either hesitate and rarely prune or they prune with carefree abandon. Both approaches can be successful or disastrous depending on the plant, but it's more important to know that regular pruning can benefit both the plants and the gardener. Pruning promotes the health of a plant, tree, or shrub, while adding to the overall aesthetics of your garden and yard.

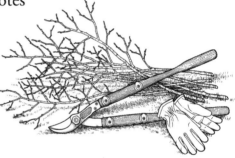

Why We Prune

As gardeners, we prune to exert some influence in the garden and shape the growth of our cherished plants. There's often an unmistakable look of satisfaction on a gardener's face when their garden has been tidied by pruning. The same experience is often had when a fruit or nut tree bears with abundance after a proper pruning, or when the uneven canopy of a shade tree fills in as a result of a pruning.

Most plants, trees, and shrubs will display their appreciation for pruning with healthy, balanced growth. For the plant, regular pruning can make it stronger and more able to resist high winds, ice storms, and snow damage. Without pruning, many plants can fall victim to disease or may suffer from crowding too much growth.

In Nature, the wind and gravity (with the help of some animals, such as raccoons) carelessly tear shoots and branches from plants. Whether these wounds heal properly or not is left to chance. We can—dare it be written—do a better job of pruning on a plant-by-plant basis than Nature's more random course.

Once you begin pruning, the most noticeable change will be in your confidence. With every season of spring and summer pruning, you'll be better equipped and more at ease with the task. And your confidence will carry over to other gardening chores like composting, propagation, and even watering.

FIRST CRAFT, THEN ART

Contrary to popular opinion, pruning is a simple craft that any gardener can easily learn and, with diligent practice, raise to an artistic form. Armed with the information in this book and a rudimentary set of tools, you can happily prune for the rest of your life.

The basic craft of pruning starts with how to make a cut that protects the plant from invasive diseases and promotes natural healing. Knowing when during the year to cut for desired effects will greatly increase your chances for success. It's also helpful to know when not to prune. Shaping young shoots, laterals, and branches for better growth or greater bloom by bending, tying, weighting, or spreading—without making a single cut—is a "new," efficient way to train young plants so they need much less pruning as they mature.

When each cut causes doubt or worry, pruning becomes a daunting venture and a far cry from art. Don't fret. Plants have a remarkable life force—they very seldom die outright from a so-called "butchered" pruning job. They have many miraculous ways of healing themselves, and pruning mistakes can often be easily fixed the very same season or the following year or two.

Many gardeners have declared "Pruning is an *Art*." Yet the real art of pruning is in the eyes of the pruner. Most times, all a gardener needs is a bit of craftsmanship to properly prune—like a good haircut at a barber versus an expensive "styling" at a hair salon. Both the trim and the styling get the job done. But the fancier the cut, the higher the price. Likewise, shearing a swan-shaped boxwood topiary takes *at least* three times more effort than trimming a simple boxwood hedge. The skill or art required for topiary is definitely more advanced, but do not let the art of pruning deter you from learning the simple craft first. The most successful gardeners mix solid pruning with flashes of artistry to great effect.

Pruning confidence, along with nuances and refinements, will come with practice. Once you learn how to identify a plant's basic anatomy and growth habits, it's possible to prune it correctly without even knowing its name. In a short time, pruning becomes as reflexive as raking leaves or turning a compost pile. Then, pruning is an instinctive way to help your garden flourish and the art can follow later, as you wish.

A New Look at Pruning

A new approach to pruning is espoused in this book. Like any science, horticulture has progressed steadily over the years, and the methods recommended in plant pruning today are a far cry from what was taught five, ten, or twenty years ago. Gone are the days of flush cuts, pruning tars and paint, topping, and pruning only in spring.

Learning to prune is much less daunting when you understand the tenets of plant anatomy and growth. If you learn such basic terms as shoots, laterals, branches, limbs, root suckers, and tip buds, your maiden voyage in pruning will be much smoother. The botany behind pruning—how a plant's internal messages, passed along by hormones, direct plant growth—is fundamental to the "new" method of pruning and will give you an advantage when faced with unfamiliar plants, shrubs, or trees.

Among other conventions redefined here will be when to prune. Besides the traditional time of dormant spring—summer, fall, and, in some climates, winter are perfectly acceptable times to engage in pruning. And in the spirit of new developments in pruning, the latest and greatest tools will be examined in detail, with particular attention paid to stress-reducing designs and new safety precautions.

Nowhere does the "new" philosophy of pruning resonate louder then when referring to cutting and shaping (placing young shoots in a position for growth, fruitfulness, or both—without using a pruning shear). The correct approach to pruning emphasizes cutting and shaping in the early years of a plant's development; very little pruning will be necessary at maturity when these two methods are used in combination throughout a plant's infancy.

Once you master the basics, you're ready for the pruning details on your favorite plants. The latter half of this book is an illustrated directory to a wide range of plants (organized in lists by common name first, for ease of reference), from perennial daisies and shady oak trees to flowering shrubs, vines, and highly trained espalier fruit trees. Before-and-after illustrations should help alleviate some of the apprehension of applying what you've learned. The plants are grouped by categories, broken down by deciduous and evergreen varieties, and list after list of appropriate plants are included.

The right mix of knowledge, confidence, and experience will make you sure-handed at the craft and art of pruning in no time. Keep this book in easy reach as a quick reminder during day-to-day gardening.

A Pruner's Lexicon *to* How Plants Work

Most garden plant growth needs pruning. But sorting out all the options about where and when to cut is the reason why so many gardeners cringe at the thought of taking clippers to plant. The seemingly simple business of pruning becomes extremely complicated and disquieting when faced with an overgrown mass of a plant. Where do you begin?

Observation is the best education for the would-be pruner. By mimicking observed growth habits, you can learn to shape and control plants along the same lines that occur naturally. Plant growth is predetermined; pruning merely augments and tries to direct the inevitable.

Knowing some fundamentals about plants and plant growth establishes a permanent foundation on which to build a sturdy framework of pruning skills. Plants grow according to the programming embedded in their cells. Their reactions to pruning, by you or otherwise, are instinctive and become very predictable to the trained eye. Thus, learning the basics of plant anatomy is the first step. But understanding how all the parts of a plant work together will unlock the true mystery of pruning, allowing you to make sense of why, where, and when you're cutting. Soon, you may find that your pruning becomes almost second nature. As your comfort level increases, you'll be ready to try more advanced methods of pruning, like espalier.

Part of what makes pruning so difficult to learn is the terminology; it appears overwhelming at first, but it is quite simple once you master the basics. Various horticultural professionals use different terms to describe the same thing. Arborists (professionals concerned with the planting and care of shrubs, trees, and vines) use different terms than orchardists, and landscape architects have their own lingo, too.

PLANT BASICS

All plants are not alike—that's plain to see. American desert cacti are quite different from New England sugar maples. Tiny tundra plants of the arctic plains and coastal, boggy cranberry shrubs appear to be distant relatives at best. Still, many plants in your garden developed along the same evolutionary path and thus have shared features. Learning the commonalities among plants will make you a better pruner, one who is often able to prune without even knowing a plant's name.

ROOTS: Roots, the underground anchor for all plants, absorb moisture and mineral nutrients from the soil to help feed the plant (shoots, laterals, branches, limbs, and trunk[s]) above ground. The roots send the gathered moisture and nutrients to these portions via the *xylem*, which on shrubs and trees is a thin layer of cells adjacent to the woody part of the stem or trunk. The food energy gathered by the leaves is transported down to feed the roots via the *phloem*, a thin layer of cells just beneath the bark. Herbaceous perennials have xylem and phloem cells arranged throughout or around the stem in columns called *vascular bundles*. Roots also store some of the nutrients generated by the leaves and make chemical compounds that help regulate the growth of the foliage.

ROOT STRUCTURE: Root systems can be described as either *fibrous* or *taprooted*. Except for oaks, conifers, and some desert plants, most trees and shrubs—regardless of how they're pruned—naturally have a fibrous root system, which is characterized by many major horizontal roots (*laterals*) with vertical roots (*sinker roots*) originating at various points along the laterals.

More herbaceous perennials than shrubs, vines, and trees have true taproots, which are thick, fleshy, carrotlike roots that travel deep in the soil and have smaller roots growing up and down the length of the root; taprooted trees are not that common in home gardens.

The root system of most plants, shrubs, or trees is much wider and more extensive than commonly assumed. Typically, a properly planted shrub or tree will, after growing for a season or two, have roots one-half again wider than the foliage (*canopy*) of the plant in heavy clay soils, and three or more times wider than the canopy in sandy soils. This means that watering and mulching should take place primarily outside the edge of the canopy.

ROOTS AND TIP GROWTH: Besides gathering and storing food

SUCKERS

Suckers are undesirable growth originating from the lower portion of the stem or roots of a woody plant. Since many plants are grafted (when the top part, or *scion*, of the plant has been grown on a different rootstock, to control the habit of the plant) onto different rootstocks, any growth that originates from the roots will have different, often undesirable foliage, flower, or fruit characteristics. Suckers primarily grow from below the soil, in the root system. These shoots grow quickly and can soon tower above the canopy of young plants unless checked. For example, certain Oriental pear rootstocks form root systems that can tolerate heavy, clay-based soils, but if a sucker is allowed to grow and bear, the fruits are small, hard, and mealy tasting. The suckers from hybrid tea roses, for example, usually develop into rank-growing plants with inferior, smaller flowers.

for the plant, roots work in conjunction with the rest of the plant to direct growth. Pruning done aboveground can affect the way the roots function. By understanding the interplay between roots and the rest of the plant, your pruning can work with a plant's desire to force new growth each spring using stored food.

A good example of a natural root dynamic occurs each spring when the tiny root hairs in the soil begin to grow before any leaves sprout. You can see this at a nursery that carries deciduous bare-root plants. Pull some plants out of their sawdust and watch how quickly the pale pink-and-white root hairs grow over a month's time.

This developmental sequence is necessary because the tiny root hairs, which gather mineral nutrients and moisture from the soil, have to be well established before the leaves require nutrients and moisture. (The roots begin their growth by using stored food.) Remarkably, the buds at the tip of the branches—far from the soil—start the root hair growth with a chemical signal moving down the plant.

LEAVES AND PHOTOSYNTHESIS: For plants, trees, and shrubs, leaves are the food-producing "factories." They come in all shapes and sizes, from round needles and pointed, palm-shaped leaves to the odd-shaped geranium leaves or the elliptical leaves of a boxwood. Some plants, like brooms (*Cytisus* spp.), have very few true leaves and use their stems for food production.

SAP

Sap is the liquid that circulates in plants through the xylem and phloem. It is composed primarily of amino acids (the building blocks of protein), food from photosynthesis, water, and sugars. Of paramount importance to the pruner, sap is used to send the chemical messages, including hormones, which bring about and control all plant growth.

Leaves contain chlorophyll and use it, along with water and CO_2, to convert light into plant food through a process called *photosynthesis*. Science can explain in detail what happens chemically, but most of us take it on faith. More importantly though, through this manufacturing process, sugars, cellulose, and starches are produced.

As plants mature, their "body" (tissue) grows and is capable of storing increasingly more food. During the summer, leaves produce food for storage in all portions of the plant's tissues to build up reserves for next spring's growth, and to repair injuries to the plant. Most of the carbohydrates are stored in the branches nearest the leaves.

CANOPIES: The foliage of a tree or shrub is its *canopy*. This term is used for all woody plants. Depending on the type of tree and its natural habit, there are three major canopy styles—round, pyramidal, and vertical. A tree's canopy is a product of its scaffold (branch system) shape and is thus determined in the first few years of growth. The term "canopy" is often used interchangeably with "crown," which is slightly different, referring to the entire upper portion of the tree from the bottom of the scaffold to the highest bud.

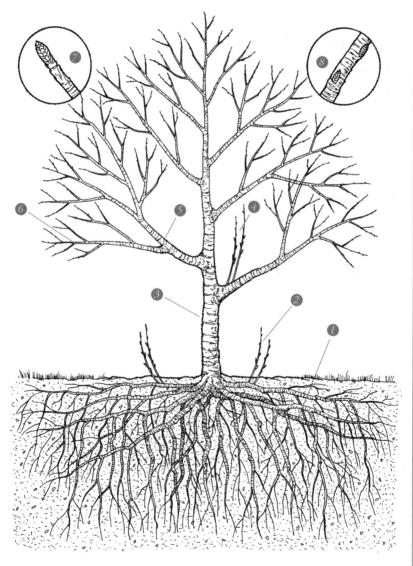

Understanding pruning begins with learning the parts of the tree.

1. Roots	3. Trunk	5. Limb	7. Tip bud
2. Suckers	4. Watersprouts	6. Branch	8. Shoot

CROSSING BRANCHES

There's nothing wrong with two shoots, branches, or limbs that cross near each other. The danger comes when two crossed branches rub against one another and cause a permanent uncallused wound. There is a chance that the open lesion can be an entry point for pests and diseases. It's prudent to remove one of the crossing branches as soon as you notice it and allow the wound to callus.

STEMS AND TRUNKS: Perennial plants, shrubs, and young trees all have stems, but the type of tissue varies considerably between herbaceous perennials and woody plants. Herbaceous perennials have stalks of soft tissue that are somewhat rigid but not truly woody. The phloem is found in the vascular bundles, like long strands of conductive tissue, in connection with the xylem. These vascular bundles form the major supports of herbaceous stems.

Woody plants have young shoots, branches, limbs, and trunks with *sapwood*—active xylem that transports the water and nutrients—just under the bark. The mature xylem or *heartwood* maintains the plant's structural strength and fights the invasion of rot and infections. Heartwood is usually darker than sapwood and forms the annual rings.

SHOOTS AND LATERALS: *Shoot* is a specific term used by arborists for one-year-old, unbranched growth. A *lateral*, often called a side shoot, is technically (in arborist's terminology) a shoot growing in any direction from a "parent" branch (meaning older growth). Fruit growers often use lateral to refer to a young shoot that's unbranched and growing more to the side and less upright.

BRANCHES: Shoots will eventually grow into branches. A *branch* is two- to four-year-old growth connected to the trunk (primary scaffold or leader), and is still capable of growing new shoots and laterals.

BRANCH COLLAR: A *branch collar* is a swollen or shoulderlike lump at the base of a stem or branch (or limb) where it attaches to the trunk, another branch, or another limb. Within the branch collar is an area with special cells and chemicals to prevent the spread of decay or pathogens. This process, called *compartmentalization*, traps destructive diseases and decay, preventing their spread into the interior of the woody plant. As a branch begins to die naturally, the branch collar becomes more conspicuous. Understanding the function of the branch collar is instrumental to proper pruning of all woody plants.

BRANCH BARK RIDGE: The *branch bark ridge* is the darkened or raised portion of bark in the crotch of a tree or shrub that denotes where the wood of a branch meets the wood of the trunk.

LIMBS: Again, limbs are more precisely defined by arborists. A *limb* is more than four years old, no longer branches, and is part of the permanent structure of the tree.

BUDS

B roadly speaking, pruning is done to encourage or limit the growth of plants. In many cases, it is done to stimulate the production of flowers, fruit, or new shoots to improve the overall shape of a plant. Most new growth begins with buds, and your understanding of them is pivotal to successful pruning. There are different types of buds—tip buds, dormant buds, leaf and flower buds, trace buds, and spurs—that should be treated differently depending on the desired result.

DORMANT BUDS: *Dormant buds* can become either a shoot (vegetative growth) or a flower bud (flowering and/or fruiting growth). Dormant pruning is done in the late winter or early spring before the flowers or leaves show. Here, the word "dormant" means that the bud is inactive and hasn't developed into either a shoot or a flower bud. Dormant buds grow along each one-year-old

WATERSPROUTS

W *atersprouts* are shoots that can grow from any part of the tree above the soil. They are characterized by rapid growth that is long, spindly, and vertical. This "weedy" growth can be forced when pruning large, older branches and limbs, but naturally grows without provocation from some trees. Watersprouts tend to grow fast.

On young trees, they have the potential to become sturdy, healthy branches, ornamental flowering shoots, or fruitful branches.

shoot (the current summer's growth) and are tucked away between the base of each new leaf's stem and the shoot on both evergreen and deciduous plants. With deciduous plants, the leaves fall off before winter and reveal that the dormant buds were at the base of each leaf-stem. These inactive buds can be found staggered alternately around and along the stem, or as whorls spaced at regular intervals.

TIP BUDS: The *tip bud* (also called apical bud, terminal bud, or leader bud) is the large, fat bud perched on the tip of each shoot. The tip bud maintains its position above other shoots because the highest bud sends a hormonal signal down the shoot to stop all dormant buds from sprouting. At the same time, the tip bud continues its vigorous growth.

The dominance of a tip bud is dependent on its position in relation to other buds. The most vertically growing shoots have a more stifling influence on lower dormant buds than a tip bud growing at a 45° angle. A tip bud growing at a horizontal angle has lost virtually all of its chemical control; most of the dormant buds "awaken" to become new vertical shoots and nearly all growth of the original tip bud will stop.

If the one-year-old growth is very long and there are no side laterals, then the tree has strong tip dominance over the lower dormant buds. If there are some laterals and flower blossoms on the two-year-old growth, the tip bud has diminished dominance. Shoots with a strong tip bud require harder pruning (by cutting farther back into last season's growth), encouraging laterals to grow where you want them. If the plant is already inclined to make laterals, lighter pruning achieves the same effect.

The effects of tip-bud dominance can be observed by tying down selected laterals or branches in the summer to various angles, observing the results. (These are not ubiquitous rules, but general concepts with plenty of exceptions. The foliage of weeping trees, for example, cascades down, thus disobeying the principle discussed here.)

LEAF VS. FLOWER BUDS: Not all the food made in the leaves makes its way down to the roots. Some food is stored in dormant buds along new shoots. These dormant buds can become either leaf (vegetative) buds or flower buds. *Leaf buds* sprout a leaf or grow into shoots. Flower buds tend to be fatter and are located close to the base of the

HOW PLANT GROWTH IS DETERMINED BY HORMONES AND STORED FOOD

All plants use stalks, stems, shoots, branches, limbs, and trunks as conduits for hormonal signals, or "memos," that stimulate some parts of the plant to grow and others to remain still. Since hormones induce growth, working with their natural patterns is the key to being a smart, efficient pruner.

The tip bud (the highest bud on each shoot) produces two important hormones; one encourages the shoot to grow vertically and the other prevents dormant buds below the tip bud from producing shoots that will compete with it. This dynamic is called *tip-bud dominance*. The same hormone that inhibits growth of buds below the tip bud also represses the tendency of all horizontal branches to curve upward and compete with the tip-bud, thus leading to a more spreading tree.

Each shoot's growth is encouraged or constrained by a constant chemical signal. By removing the tip bud, you will eliminate tip-bud dominance, thereby stimulating dormant buds to grow into shoots and laterals. Conversely, leaving the tip bud uncut allows you to control the width of the plant and encourage greater vertical growth.

Removing tip buds is not the only way to encourage growth. Leaves on any branch produce food to be stored for next spring's growth. If you cut four feet off the end of a branch for example, stored food still wants to return from where it came the following spring. Since there are no tip buds to constrain shoot growth, there is often a riot of new growth where the branch was cut.

The results of pruning are often dependent on the vitality of the plant, which is related to the amount of stored food. A vigorous plant will produce more new shoots below each cut than a poorly growing plant. Over time, you will be able to anticipate how many shoots to expect after each cut.

previous season's growth. Young flower buds usually have more stored carbohydrates than leaf buds. By the end of summer, flower buds look visibly more rotund than typical dormant buds. In fact, by early fall, all the pollen is already formed inside tiny flowers within the buds.

A cluster of buds on a shoot or branch can have both leaf and flower buds. Peach trees have a little triumvirate of buds that bloom (although it's not uncommon for single buds to bloom). The typical cluster of three peach buds has two fat flower buds on the outside and a slim leaf bud in the middle.

TRACE BUDS: *Trace buds* (also called latent buds) are the withered remains of a dormant bud that didn't grow. Located along a shoot, lateral, or branch of a shrub or a tree, trace buds are wrinkled, eye-shaped creases that are easy to spot on growth up to four years old. Older branches may have faint imprints of where buds used to be, but the crease will be a single curved line, or "wink." Cutting just above a trace bud will stimulate new shoots or laterals below it. Locating and cutting above a trace bud is an extremely easy and efficient way to fill in parts of the scaffold that are bare.

As limbs get even older, all hint of the trace buds is absorbed into the bark; however, they are relatively close together along the length of a branch or limb. Thus, cutting just about anywhere will reawaken a "sleeping" dormant bud, except with shrubs and trees that will not make new shoots from old, bare branches or limbs. Skilled pruners can show you what a trace bud looks like on your trees. And unlike other methods of pruning, stimulating trace buds is an effective way to ensure new growth where you want it.

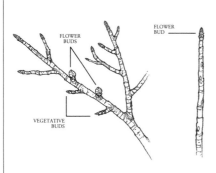

Branches growing from the trunk at a 45° angle are well positioned for developing flower buds. Upright stems tend to grow tall, with little or no flowering.

FLOWERING

Part of what makes the spring special is the profusion of flowers from trees and shrubs. Each spring, the fattening and eventual bloom of flower buds on trees and shrubs indicates the beginning of the growing season. As the years pass, your flowering plants can become less productive, often with blooms and fruit farther out on branches. Pruning can help keep your treasured flowering plants in healthy, well-balanced bloom if you understand that plants have a different method of flowering. In many cases, limb position and the age of the bud-producing shoot are the determining factor.

BUD AND LIMB POSITION: When assessing the flowering or fruitfulness of your trees and shrubs, good bud and limb position is everything. A shoot's growth is proportional to its position. The most

TERMINAL-FLOWERING TREES AND SHRUBS

American yellowwood
 (*Cladrastis lutea*)
Amur maackia (*Maackia amurensis*)
Athel Tree, Tamarix
 (*Tamarix aphylla*)
Avocado (*Persea americana*)
Black locust (*Robinia pseudoacacia*)
Buckeyes (*Aesculus* spp.)
Butterfly Bush, common
 (*Buddleia davidii*)
Catalpa (*Catalpa bignonioies*)
Catalpa, Northern / Western
 (*C. speciosa*)
Cherimoya (*Annona cherimola*)
Chestnut, Chinese
 (*Castanea mollissima*)
Chestnut, Spanish (*C. sativa*)
Chinese flame tree
 (*Koelreuteria bipinnata*)
Crape myrtle (*Lagerstroemia indica*)
Figs (*Ficus carica*)
Gardenia (*Gardenia jasminoides*)
Goldenrain tree
 (*Koelreuteria paniculata*)
Grapes (*Vitis* spp.)
Hibiscus, Chinese, tropical
 (*Hibiscus rosa-sinensis*)
Hydrangea (*Hydranga arborescens*)
Loquat (*Eriobotrya japonica*)

Macadamia (*Macadamia* spp.)
Magnolia trees and shrubs
 (*Magnolia* spp.)
Mango (*Mangifera indica*)
Maples (*Acer* spp.)
Medlar (*Mespilus germanica*)
Mountain papaya (*Carica pubescens*)
Natal plum (*Carissa macrocarpa*)
Oleander (*Nerium oleander*)
Olive (*Olea europaea*)
Oranges, Lemons, all other Citrus
 (*Citrus* spp.)
Persimmon, American
 (*Diospyros virginiana*)
Persimmon, Japanese
 (*D. kaki*)
Pineapple guava (*Feijoa sellowiana*)
Quince (*Cydonia oblonga*)
Roses (*Rosa* spp.)
Rugosa rose (*Rosa rugosa*)
Spirea (*Spiraea* spp.)
Spirea, Japanese (*S. japonica*)
Strawberry/Lemon guava
 (*Psidium cattleianum*)
Summersweet, Sweet pepperbush
 (*Clethra alnifolia*)
Walnuts and Butternut
 (*Juglans* spp.)
White sapote (*Casimiroa edulis*)

vertical-growing shoots will usually grow with the most vigor. Those laterals that are horizontal or below horizontal exhibit the least amount of seasonal growth; all shoots that are angled in between will have growth relative to the two extremes.

LIMB POSITION FOR FLOWERS: As a general guideline, the best position for a shoot to naturally favor lateral growth and some flower buds—whether on ornamental or fruit trees—is between 45° and 60° (although there are numerous exceptions depending on the tree's natural—genetically controlled—growth habit). Some of the tip bud's influence is lost because of the angled branching, so flowering and new branching are encouraged. A reasonable amount of tip growth should remain so the plant continues to increase its overall size. Pruning or shaping new growth to this ideal zone of position (45°–60°) will promote more laterals without extra pruning. Also, the stimulation of flower buds yields greater ornamental beauty and, with food crops, more bounty to harvest.

Terminal-flowering shoots on plants like quince, bloom after the tip of a stem begins to grow.

FLOWERING SHOOTS: When pruning for healthy bloom, first- or second-year shoots will be the focus of your attention. There are a number of different shoot-flowering habits. Again, careful observation of the different methods that shoots employ to produce bloom will help you understand how to prune them. There are, of course, commonalities among all flowering shoots.

TERMINAL-FLOWERING SHOOTS: Plants that bloom only once on the current year's growth are called *terminal-flowering* (terminal-bearing, for fruit and nut trees) plants. Terminal-flowering plants are easy to spot. The tip bud begins to grow in spring, followed by leafy, vegetative growth for several inches along the shoot, and then a flower bud forms and blooms at the end of the short, new shoot.

Terminal-flowering plants offer the pruner two options: if the plant

SECOND-YEAR-FLOWERING TREES AND SHRUBS

Beatrix Farrand
  (*Forsythia intermedia*)
Beauty bush
  (*Kolkwitzia amabilis*)
Bramble, Blackberry
  (*Rubus allegheniensis*)
Bramble, Rocky Mountain
  Thimbleberry (*R. deliciosus*)
Cream bush, Ocean Spray
  (*Holodiscus discolor*)
Currant, Alpine
  (*Ribes alpinum*)
Currant, Missouri or Buffalo
  (*R. odoratum*)
Currant, Red-flowering
  (*R. sanguineum*)
Deutzia (*Deutzia scabra*)
Deutzia, Showy (*D. magnifica*)
Deutzia, Slender (*D. gracilus*)

Forsythia, Weeping
  (*Forsythia suspensa*)
Forsythia, White
  (*Abeliophyllum distichum*)
Jasmine, Dwarf shrub
  (*Jasminum parkeri*)
Jasmine, Primrose shrub (*J. mesnyi*)
Lilac (*Syringa microphylla*)
Peach (*Prunus persica*)
Raspberry, Red (summer fruiting)
  (*Rubus strigosus, R. idaeus*)
Showy border forsythia,
  Goldenbells
  (*Forsythia intermida* 'Spectabilis')
Sweet or Fragrant Mock Orange
  (*Philadelphus coronarius*)
Tamarisk (*Tamarix african*)
Tamarisk (spring flowering)
  (*T. parviflora*)

is never pruned, there are always plenty of blooms; if the plant is pruned severely, but some of last year's shoots and laterals are uncut, there will still be blooms.

Terminal-flowering plants are partially or fully leafed-out before flowering begins. The fruiting members of this group of plants make low-maintenance espaliers—vigorous pruning will not ruin the harvest and no pruning still results in good yields.

SECOND-YEAR-FLOWERING SHOOTS: Some trees and shrubs must save up energy in dormant buds for an entire growing season

Some plants, such as peaches, flower on shoots that were produced the previous growing season.

SUMMER-FLOWERING TREES AND SHRUBS

Bluebeard (*Caryopteris* spp.)

Butterfly bush, common
(*Buddleia* spp.)

Cape fuchsia (*Phygelius capensis*)

Fuchsia, hybrid (*Fuchsia hybrida*)

Honeysuckle bush, southern
(*Diervilla sessilifolia*)

Hydrangea (*Hydrangea arborescens*)

Hydrangea, Peegee
(*Hydrangea paniculata*)

Indigo (*Indigofera incarnata*)

Lilacs, deciduous summer or wild
(*Ceanothus* spp.)

Lupine, Coastal bush
(*Lupinus arboreus*)

Plumbago, Dwarf
(*Ceratostigma plumbaginoides*)

Sage, Jerusalem
(*Phlomis fruticosa*)

Sage, Russian
(*Perovskia atriplicifolia*)

Spanish broom (*Spartium junceum*)

Spicebush (*Calycanthus* spp.)

Tree mallow
(*Lavatera assurgentiflora*)

Verbena, Lemon (*Aloysia triphylla*)

---

to make flower buds. With *second-year-flowering plants*, the current spring's bloom comes on last year's growth; thus, bloom occurs only once at each spot on the branch. Such plants are identified by large, fat buds on the lower half of one-year-old shoots in late summer or on two-year-old branches early in the following spring. Three-year-old branches will have few, if any, fat flower buds left from the previous season.

Second-year-flowering plants are constantly producing flowers farther and farther from their center because new growth must occur for the one-time flowering. If flowering (or fruiting) is desired near the center of the plant instead of at the outer reaches of the foliage, reasonable yearly pruning is required. Without the removal of up to 50% of the yearly growth, the new growth will be farther from the ground and middle of the canopy with each passing season. If these plants are neglected, they may continue to bloom profusely, but only in a thin layer at the outer edge of the canopy, which will probably be shaped like an umbrella or thimble.

SUMMER-FLOWERING SHOOTS: Plants that make new shoot growth in the spring to store up enough food for blooming in the summer and through the fall are called *summer-flowering plants*, and many herbaceous perennials and flowering shrubs fit into this category. These plants will bloom every year without pruning. Summer-flowering plants have two drawbacks: the bloom on woody shrubs gets farther away from the middle of the plant without pruning; and they easily build up plenty of shabby-looking or dead shoots because they have already bloomed.

SPUR-TYPE FLOWERING: Plants with *spur-type flowering* are easily identified by their telltale spur clusters. These plants are more unforgiving the first year than previously mentioned plants; miss the first season's pruning and you'll have to work much harder on the second-year's growth to encourage flower formation. As a pruner, you should realize that once the first season's work has been done, the plant rewards the pruner with repeated bloom at the same place on the limb—sometimes for decades.

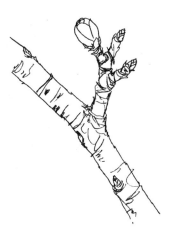

As the seasons pass, the initial flower bud often "branches" out into a collection of tiny shoots with a flower bud at each tip or cluster of multiple flower buds. Once a flowering spot on an ornamental or fruit tree branch has more than one flower bud, it is often called a spur or spur system. The multiplication of flower

Apple trees flower on short stems called spurs, or spur systems.

buds—on little shootlike growth or in whorls (clusters) of buds—means flowering is insured each year at the same location. Apple and pear trees as well as wisteria vines have classic branched spur systems.

SPUR SYSTEMS: A *spur system* begins, as all blossoms do, as a single-flowering bud (from a dormant bud) on an ornamental or fruiting tree, shrub, or vine. They are called systems because the flower buds develop into clusters on a short branching growth. Spur systems often have more leaves in a whorl around the bud instead of a singular leaf like a dormant bud. Many ornamental and fruiting trees, as well as some shrubs and vines, must take a season to divert all the proper foods and hormones to convert dormant buds into young flower buds on second-year shoots. Spur-type plants are unique because they continue to flower at the same

SPUR-FLOWERING TREES, SHRUBS, AND VINES

Actinidia (Chinese), Yangtao
  (*Actinidia chinensis*)
Almond (*Prunus amygdalus*)
Almond, Dwarf flowering*
  (*P. glandulosa*)
Almond, Flowering* (*P. triloba*)
Apple (*Malus* spp.)
Apple (*M. pumila*)
Apricot (*Prunus armeniaca*)
**Cherry, Birchbark or Japanese
  Flowering*** (*P. serrulata*)
**Cherry, Manchu or Nanking
  Cherry** (*P. tomentosa*)
Cherry, Sargent* (*P. sargentii*)
Cherry, Sour or Pie (*P. cerasus*)
Cherry, Sweet (*P. avium*)
Cherry, Western sand (*P. besseyi*)
Crab apple* (*Malus rosaceae*)
Crab apple* (*M. tschonoskii*)
Crab apple, Siberian*
  (*M. baccata*)
**Gooseberry, Red, White and
  Black Currants** (*Ribes* spp.)
Grape, Concord Seedless
  (*Vitis labrusca*)

**Grape, European or Flame
  Seedless** (*V. vinifera*)
Kiwi (fuzzy) (*Actinidia deliciosa*)
Kiwi, cold-hardy (smooth skin)
  (*A. arguta*)
Pear, Asian and Ussurian*
  (*Pyrus ussuriensis*)
Pear, Callery* (*P. calleryana*)
Pear, European (*P. communis*)
Pear, Evergreen* (*P. kawakamii*)
Pear, Japanese sand* (*P. pyrifolia*)
Pear, Weeping willow-leafed*
  (*P. salicifolia*)
Plum, Cherry
  (*Prunus cerasifera*)
Plum, Dwarf Red-Leaf*
  (*P. cistena*)
Plum, European Blue Damson
  (*P. domestica*)
Plum, Flowering* (*P. blireiana*)
Plum, Redleaf*
  (*P. cerasifera* 'Thundercloud')
Wisteria, Chinese*
  (*Wisteria sinesis*)
Wisteria, Japanese (*W. floribunda*)

*Ornamental plants

spot on the branch or limb for many years thereafter—whether they're a fruiting or an ornamental plant.

Not all flower buds on spur systems bloom every year; some buds bloom, while others are storing up enough food energy to bloom in the subsequent spring. The buds alternate blooming, but each spur system continues to flower and make fruit each season. The process of off-year bud regeneration allows for productive spur clusters year after year. The reliabilty of spur flowering (and fruit production) makes spur-producing plants desirable.

Tree Shapes

Since trees are usually the focal points of any garden or larger property, they get the bulk of pruning attention—especially when they're young. Trees are also an investment in time, money, and effort.

Trees will naturally grow into a variety of shapes, and the pruner's job is to guide a tree's natural shape so it is strong, healthy, and aesthetically pleasing. A tree's first set of permanent branches, or scaffold, should be chosen with care. It's important to know which shape you want for a tree before you plant it. This way, you'll avoid heavy pruning later to control growth. It's also very important to be aware of a tree's potential size *before* you plant it. Consider the area where you want to plant the tree. At maturity, how big will the tree be? Will it shade parts of the garden, lawn, or house? Will it grow into power lines? Tree shape choices are often made on the basis of aesthetics or what is healthiest for the tree. But a tree that has outgrown its location is a hazard regardless of the scaffold shape you choose.

Decurrent and Excurrent Crowns: Most trees naturally grow a crown, which is the limbs and branches of a tree or shrub's upper portion from the lowest on the trunk to the highest, that's either decurrent or excurrent. Trees with wide, rounded crowns with many tip buds competing for the dominant position are called *decurrent* trees. These trees have weak tip-bud dominance because numerous shoots have grown to the same height at the top of the crown. Decurrent trees will usually have more than one trunk at a certain point above the ground.

Trees that naturally maintain one trunk up through the entire height of the crown are called *excurrent*. These trees have strong tip-bud dominance at the top of the central trunk. Few side-shoots ever have a chance to compete with the tip bud of the trunk. Excurrent trees grow like Christmas trees—a single trunk up the middle and an overall pyramidal shape to the branches and foliage.

Primary and Secondary Scaffold Shapes: The term scaffold, which refers to the main limbs or permanent structure for all other branches, laterals, and shoots, applies only to trees and is used frequently by fruit tree growers. The primary scaffold is formed in the first few years of a tree's life. Thereafter, it is difficult to form new limbs as a part of the primary scaffold—although it's quite easy to remove any of the primary scaffold's limbs with summer pruning. The next series or level of branching from the primary scaffold is called the secondary scaffold.

STANDARD SCAFFOLD: Nurserymen or landscapers create a *standard* scaffold by pruning away all the lower limbs to a 5'–8' level on the

Productive fruit trees are generally trained into central leader (above left), modified or delayed central leader (above right), or open center (below left), which encourage strong, fruitful growth.

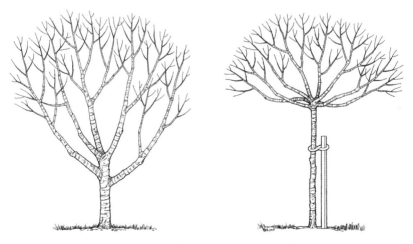

Open-center trees—as they grow older—can grow structurally weak. Standard-shape trees (lower right) are largely an invention of the landscape trade.

trunk. This style is mostly an invention of the landscape trade, but many nurseries and gardeners subject trees to this form. If the scaffold is naturally round, the result of pruning in this style is a decurrent tree that looks like a lollipop. With an excurrent tree, it looks like a Christmas tree stuck on top of a stick. (However, this style does mimic what happens to the lower limbs in a crowded forest as increasing shade causes lower branches to wither.)

Central Leader Scaffold: Orchardists use the term, *central leader* scaffold to describe a tree with a single trunk up the middle. The "central leader" is the dominant vertical shoot that forms the center trunk and is usually located on the highest part of the main trunk. Arborists prefer the term "excurrent."

The limbs on a central leader tree radiate at a wide or narrow angle of attachment up the trunk. To maintain the tip dominance on fruit trees so they don't get too tall for pruning and harvesting, each tree must be grafted (when the top part, or *scion*, of the plant has been grown on a different rootstock, to control the habit of the plant). If the leader is cut back each spring to force side shoots and a new leader is regrown, this is called a *modified central leader* tree. Both sizes of these trees have a pyramidal shape; the characteristic growth is typical of the traditional Christmas tree—triangular.

Even if you plan to prune off the lower limbs of a central leader tree to make a standard scaffold, it's best to leave them on for at least a few seasons. Trunks that have retained their limbs to the ground nearly always have a bigger diameter compared to the same age tree that had all its lower limbs pruned off at planting time.

Open-Center Scaffold: Commonly used with fruit trees, open-center scaffolds are a result of the leader being removed at dormant planting time in an effort to control the height of these vigorous trees (grafted to full-size rootstocks). Then, three to five main branches are trained to grow at wide angles from the trunk in order to favor width over height. Unfortunately, the main limbs all grow from a very short trunk, which can cause serious problems as the tree matures. As the tree ages, each limb's weight is farther from the trunk's center, which may eventually force the tree to fall apart. For long-term trees, this style is discouraged as the weight of the branches can pull the tree apart.

DELAYED OPEN-CENTER SCAFFOLD: Orchardists refer to *delayed open-center* trees as a more vigorous tree trained to have a central trunk for 3'–5' or more. Then the central leader is permanently removed with summer pruning. This technique is used to form the strong attachment of the primary scaffold to the lower portion of the trunk while encouraging a short, wide tree. The result is a canopy with a rounded pattern similar to a decurrent tree, but with less growth in the middle.

WHEN
to PRUNE

For the modern gardener, there is a reason to prune nearly every season. Unlike the old persistent myth, you *can* clip away in the spring, summer, and, in moderate-winter climates, the fall and winter. The possibility of year-round pruning is applicable to ornamentals as well as fruit and nut trees. Each season has a different set of pruning benefits and drawbacks.

Regardless of the shrub or tree, there are some simple pruning priorities: Remove dead shoots, branches, or limbs. Then remove diseased tissue; crossing shoots, laterals, branches, or limbs; weak growth; and all true suckers. As soon as you spot one of these problems, you can proceed with pruning, within reason, during just about any season.

So often the gardener is reminded to remove all dead "wood." Because herbaceous perennials don't make woody tissue as trees or shrubs do, this mandate should be: Remove any part (tissue) of the plant that's dead. By removing dead tissue immediately, it's possible to stop the progress of pests, rots, or diseases that could kill the entire plant.

Next, remove all diseased shoots, laterals, branches, or limbs. Nature has equipped most plants with various chemical zones to fight the progression of dying tissue, but they don't always succeed. Trees, for example, have a protective zone behind their branch collar that compartmentalizes rot and "walls it off" from the inner portion of the tree. In the forest, you see fallen trees with hollow trunks, proving that Nature doesn't always succeed at stopping disease and rot. Pruning before diseases travel farther back into the plant will assist Nature in curtailing diseases and rot. (Sometimes, cankers can be cut out of a branch or limb and it remains to grow, flower, and fruit.)

Two or more shoots, laterals, branches, or limbs will often cross. If the effect of rubbing causes a raw or uncallused wound, one of the two shoots should be pruned off with a thinning cut. A raw wound can allow insects or pathogens to enter the plant.

Depending on the potential size of your plant, it is best to remove any weak growth. This is, however, not a universal pruning law. If you're trying to dwarf a tree or control its height, favoring weak growth over vigorous growth, by pruning off the most vigorous parts, is to your advantage. But, if the growth is too weak, selective pruning may cause the plant to wither or die. Vigorous and weak are relative terms; practice, along with trial and error, will help you distinguish growth that is too weak or frail from growth that is merely slender or slight.

Since so many plants are grafted on rootstocks that do not have the same characteristics as the grafted plant, it's important to remove any root suckers as soon as you see them. Often, the suckers will exhibit different blooming characteristics, and can grow vigorously.

DEDUCING AGE

The wise pruner treats each year's growth differently and works with the possibilities and limitations of each. It's helpful to know the age of each piece of shoot, lateral, branch, or limb. The youngest shoots are willowy, supple, and easily influenced by the wind and the pruner alike. Older, woody growth is thick, rigid, and much more set in its ways. The trick is to identify each season's growth.

DEDUCING THE AGE OF A SHOOT: There are three ways to tell the difference between one- and two-year-old shoots and branches of deciduous trees and shrubs. (Keep in mind that these are general guidelines with many exceptions.)

First, test the limberness of a shoot. One-year-old shoots are more flexible and easier to bend into a narrow arch. If you're testing a young shoot and it snaps, the point of the break is probably near the base of the one-year-old growth. The lowest portion of a one-year-old shoot often behaves like a two-year-old branch because the plant's chemistry has already started making stiff, "woodier" cells.

Second, look for color differences between branches. A two-year-old branch usually has noticeably different color and texture compared to the previous season's growth. The colors and textures vary considerably from plant to plant. Many apple trees, for example, have light green, shiny bark on one-year-old shoots, which loses its luster and becomes more brown or darker green by the second summer. Some willows have a dull to bright orange bark on one-year-old shoots and a bark that is considerably more brown on two-year-old growth.

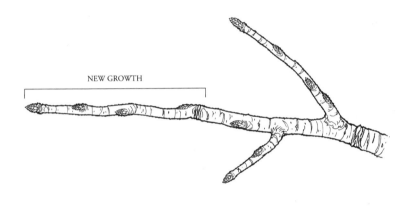

NEW GROWTH

To ascertain the ages of different parts of a branch, check variations in woodiness and color, and look closely for wrinkles that indicate where growth began in spring.

Third, check for a series of close wrinkles that look like a short stack of pancakes encircling the shoot. The wrinkles usually cover less than an inch of the length of the shoot and separate the two different colors and textures of one- and two-year-old growth. For many pruners, this method is the easiest way to tell the difference between one- and two-year-old growth.

Deducing the Age of a Branch or Limb: After the second year, most bark exhibits much less color difference between year-to-year growth. As most shoots age, the smooth, shiny young bark gets duller and begins to take on characteristics of older bark.

As with shoots, telltale clusters of wrinkles are the best way to tell the age of all older growth on deciduous shrubs and trees. After locating the wrinkles that separate the first- and second-years' growth, look down the branch or limb for other sets of wrinkles to determine the age of the branch or limb.

THE "SEASONS" OF FLOWERING

The timing of bloom on your trees and shrubs will dictate when you prune them. Flowering on most trees and shrubs occurs on the current year's growth in late spring through early summer (called terminal-flowering shoots), on the current year's growth in late summer through fall (called summer-flowering shoots), on last year's growth (called second-year-flowering shoots), or on last year's growth and for years thereafter (called spur-type flowering). Thorough observation of the plant's growth habits will reveal which type of flowering your plant exhibits.

SPRING PRUNING

Spring pruning, also called dormant or winter pruning, traditionally means cutting when there are no leaves on a deciduous tree or shrub. There are many advantages and some drawbacks to spring pruning. If you like convention, spring pruning is the most traditional time to prune. With no foliage on deciduous trees and shrubs, you can easily see what you're doing. With fruit trees and shrubs, there are no fruits or nuts on the branches to get knocked off, which might be the case with summer pruning. Spring pruning's greatest value is that branching is stimulated. If your tree is missing growth on a portion of its crown, you can cut back on growth and get new shoots.

Spring pruning is not without its drawbacks. Most new pruners find it difficult to visualize what effect their pruning is having on the summer shade patterns of deciduous plants because the leaves are missing, but experience will alleviate this problem. It's also harder to spot dead and diseased shoots, laterals, branches, or limbs when a deciduous shrub or tree is leafless. Spring pruning occasionally fosters disease problems; stimulating growth can upset the balance of nutrients in some trees and shrubs and make them more prone to disease. (In California, experience has shown that an exclusive schedule of spring pruning can encourage powdery mildew—a disease of apple, pear, and plum trees, as well as some ornamentals.) Lastly, in cold-winter areas, gloves, a warm jacket, a scarf, and a wool hat may be required, which makes moving around cumbersome and pruning awkward.

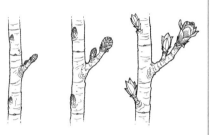

TIMING: In the coldest climates, spring pruning is done after the spring thaw, but before new leaves begin to sprout. If you're new to an area, check with established neighborhood gardeners for advice on

Spring pruning often is done when stems are still dormant. As growth begins, buds start to swell and then break open to release flowers, leaves, and shoots.

frost dates. The real trick is knowing when severe freezing is over and avoiding a late polar blast. Spring pruning is also a term that can be applied to evergreen plants because they are still "resting" before early spring growth begins. If you want to make sure you're not pruning evergreens too early, wait for the first light green new growth to insure that you escape all late frosts.

Those who live in milder climates can actually "spring" prune in mid to late winter. Mild winters allow for a long period to finish spring pruning. The best time for pruning in benign climates is simply the best weather between storms. In coastal California and southern Gulf Coast and Atlantic Ocean states, this may mean from mid November through February (or just before the flower buds begin to open).

CALENDAR DATES

In most climates, using calendar dates to define when it's safe to prune in spring is not an accurate method because you're dealing with averages. The best time to prune may vary by several weeks from one year to another. One way to determine the latest pruning date is to keep a journal or make notations on a calendar of the weather conditions and time of bloom for local flowering trees and shrubs. In a few years, you'll notice what is blooming just before your various trees and shrubs—ornamental or edible—come into leaf or bloom.

BRANCHING: Spring pruning is ideal for stimulating new branches and filling in the shape of your trees and shrubs. The more foliage and tip buds (whether it's deciduous or evergreen) pruned away, the greater the number of buds that will be stimulated into growth below the cut. Remember, after pruning tip buds, one or more buds below the first growing bud may begin to grow.

The first bud below the cut to grow quickly starts making the chemical signal to direct its growth vertically; each emerging bud's growth lags slightly behind the buds located higher on the shoot, lateral, or branch. As a result of the chemical signal from the tip bud of each higher shoot to repress competition, each sprouting bud below the first developing bud grows progressively slower. There are times when the second or third bud happens to pop out first and surpass the growth of buds higher up on the stem. Still, the highest shoots are often the longest and the lower laterals tend to be the shortest.

A TRACE OF SPRING PRUNING: If you want to make one or more shoots or laterals where no dormant buds exist, spring pruning is your answer. If there are no noticeable buds, look for trace buds. Cut above the trace bud, or the crease, where you want the first shoot or lateral. On older growth, the trace buds may not be visible, but cutting at the level on the trunk where you wish a new shoot or lateral will usually generate plenty of new shoots.

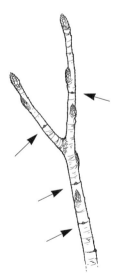

Keep in mind that some trees and shrubs will not produce shoots from bare branches. As shoots on certain plants mature, the trace buds die and can't be reawakened to make new shoots with pruning

Trace buds lie dormant on branches and may be coaxed into growing by pruning back to a point just above them.

in any season. Choose carefully which *existing* shoots or laterals to keep and which to remove.

PLANTS WITH NONPRODUCING TRACE BUDS

Even when cut in the spring, these plants don't usually make new shoots from bare lengths of stem, even though there may be what looks like trace buds. To shape the plant, cut out existing unwanted shoots, laterals, or branches to their base with thinning cuts (see page 58).

American arborvitae
(*Thuja occidentalis*)
Cedar, Atlas (*Cedrus atlantica*)
Cedar, Deodar (*C. deodara*)
Cedar, Incense and **California white** (*Calocedrus decurrens*)
Cedar, Japanese
(*Cryptomeria japonica*)
Cedar, Western Red
(*Thuga plicata* 'Aurea')
Cedar-of-Lebanon
(*Cedrus libani*)
Cypress, Bald
(*Taxodium distichum*)
Cypress, Italian
(*Cupressus sempervirens*)
Cypress, Lawson, Cedar, Port Orford
(*Chamaecyparis lawsoniana*)
Cypress, Leyland
(*Cupressocyparis leylandii*)

Cypress, Monterey
(*Cupressus macrocarpa*)
Cypress, Montezuma
(*Taxodium mucronatum*)
Fir, Balsam (*Abies balsamea*)
Fir, Douglas
(*Pseudotsuga menziesii*)
Fir, Noble (*Abies procera* 'Nobilis')
Heaths (*Erica* spp.)
Junipers (*Juniperus* spp.)
Pine, Norfolk Island
(*Araucaria heterophylla*)
Pines (*Pinus* spp.)
Rockroses (*Cistus* spp.)
Rosemary (sometimes resprouts)
(*Rosmarinus officinalis*)
Spruce, Colorado (*Picea pungens*)
Spruce, Norway (*Picea abies*)
Strawberry tree (*Arbutus unedo*)
Tea tree, Australian/New Zealand
(*Leptospermum* spp.)

SUMMER PRUNING

All the fruits of labors past come to fruition in summer, and if you're lucky, you get to sit back and enjoy some of the beautiful plant life that you've fostered. Summer is also the ideal time to rein in rampant growth (*not* encourage new growth) and prepare your prized plants, trees, and shrubs for the fall and winter to come.

Summer is an excellent time for pruning because you spread your work over a few months, unlike racing to finish your spring pruning before bloom. To get the most out of your spring growth, wait until all of the bloom from spring has died back, then reduce the size of your more vigorous trees and shrubs. In this manner, you not only get the most visual enjoyment from spring growth, but pruning in summer

What makes summer pruning distinct and practical from spring pruning is the way food is used. In summer (right), food made by photosynthesis is stored for next year's growth or to aid in callusing of pruning cuts. In spring (left), this stored food is released from the roots to encourge a flush of growth.

allows you to open up the canopy and aid growth to the interior of the plant or add a colorful blush to ripening fruit. Also, use the summer months to keep a short leash on the unwanted growth of suckers and watersprouts as they won't regrow with as much vigor in summer.

The vigor of growth changes over the seasons depending upon fertility, climate, moisture, and sunlight. Pruning late in the summer or when the plant is getting less water or rain will promote fewer shoots and laterals, which will be shorter. Gardeners in the arid West, for example, have more control over what happens during summer; the gardener can count on little or no rain to affect the plant's vigor, so new growth can be promoted or restrained by controlling the level of irrigation.

Summer is the ideal time to make more significant cuts to your trees and shrubs. With active photosynthesis, cuts quickly callus in the summer. Summer pruning affects the balance of nitrogen and reduces the suppleness of plant growth, so new growth is more resistant to diseases such as cytospora canker, powdery mildew, and bacterial blight.

The most important limitation of summer pruning is that it's unconventional and not practiced by many gardeners; it goes against the old myth that a tree will bleed to death if pruned in summer. Summer pruning is tricky for beginners because it's hard to see branching structures when a tree or shrub is in full leaf. One of the hardest adjustments to summer pruning is timing your cuts to limit, not encourage, growth. Conversely, if pruning is done too late in the summer where winters are cold, any new growth will be vulnerable to freeze damage. Making the right cut at the right time is the real challenge for novice summer pruners. Lastly, when pruning fruit trees in summer, you may knock off some fruit if pruning is done before the harvest.

THINNING THE CANOPY: Summer pruning is an excellent time to judge how much foliage you're removing. Use thinning cuts (see page 58) to remove the rampant growth as late in the summer as possible. Letting more light in through the canopy will promote healthier growth near the ground and generate more ornamental flowers and fruit lower in the tree. Using judicious cuts, leave enough foliage to protect the trunk, as well as the primary and secondary scaffolds, from getting sunburned.

In hot, dry climates like Arizona, the rules of summer pruning change to accommodate the ferocious summer heat. Native desert shrubs and trees (such as *Acacia* spp. and mesquite—*Prosopis* spp.) seem to thrive with summer pruning, and there is no risk to the exposed cut. Sunburn to the exposed trunks and limbs from the removal of too much of the crown's foliage is the main worry. When the temperatures are over 104°F, don't prune any limbs thicker than 2"; this guideline limits how much foliage is removed. In the desert, a protective, shady crown is even more important with *exotic* trees and shrubs, especially those with tender bark, like citrus trees. Your local nurseries, the Cooperative Extension Service and its Master Gardener Program, and local gardening experts and arborists can give more specific guidelines.

SUMMER PRUNING FOR SHAPE AND BLOOM: Many shrubs, whether evergreen or deciduous, need a seasonal shearing to look good

PERENNIALS AND SHRUBS NEEDING A SUMMER CLIPPING

If summer bloom comes too close to first hard freezes in cold-winter climates, some woody and soft-wooded shrubs do better if the spent flowers and uncut foliage are left for the winter. (Usually pruned after blooming.)

Azaleas, evergreen
(*Azalea* [*Rhododendron* spp.])

Candytuft, evergreen
(*Iberis sempervirens*)

Daisy, Painted Pyrethrum
(in mild climates)
(*Chrysanthemum coccineum*)

Daphne, Burkwood
(*Daphne burkwoodii*)

Daphne, February (*D. mezereum*)

Dusty miller (*Senecio cineraria*)

Euryops (*Euryops pectinatus*)

Feverfew (in mild climates)
(*Chrysanthemum parthenium*)

Heath, Biscay (*Erica mediterranea*)

Heath, Cornish (*E. vagans*)

Heath, spring (*E. carnea*)

Heath, tree (*E. arborea*)

Hebe (*H. menziesil*)

Hebe, boxleaf (*Hebe buxifolia*)

Lavender (*Lavandula* spp.)

Lilac, common (spent flowers
only) (*Syringa vulgaris*)

Lily-of-the-valley, shrub
(*Pieris japonica*)

Marguerite, blue
(*Felicia amelloides*)

Morning glory, bush
(*Convolvulus cneorum*)

Orange, Mexican (*Choisya ternata*)

Pride of Madeira (*Echium fastuosum*)

Rosemary, upright and prostrate
(*Rosmarinus* spp.)

Rue (*Ruta graveolens*)

Sage, purple (*Salvia leucophylla*)

Santolina, gray lavender cotton
(*Santolina chamaecyparissus*)

Santolina, green (*S. virens*)

Spirea (spring-flowering types only)
(*Spiraea* spp.)

Valerian, red Jupiter's beard
(*Centranthus ruber*)

Wallflower, Siberian
(*Erysimum hieraciifolium*)

Yarrow, common; Milfoil
(*Achillea millefolium*)

the following year. Since numerous shrubs bloom in mid to late summer, early summer pruning should be avoided because you'd clip off the flowers. If you leave your shrubs unpruned, each season's growth gets farther from the plant's center and the plant soon appears shaggy and rangy. Eventually, the foliage will flop open in the lightest rain or with the thinnest layer of ice or snow.

The solution is to shear back the canopy after bloom. If the crown's foliage was too rangy last summer, spare not the pruning shears. The harder you prune back the crown, the denser it will be next summer. Use a hand pruner or a hedge shearer, depending on the size of the plant.

If summer bloom comes too close to the first hard freezes in cold-winter climates, some woody shrubs fare better if the spent flowers and uncut foliage are left for the winter.

Summertime Control of Rampant Growth: If you're trying to remove unwanted, "weedy" growth, like suckers and water-sprouts, with a single pruning, then summer pruning is the best time. Limiting the plant's shoots and foliage is the purpose of summer pruning, not awakening new shoots or laterals. If you prune too early in the summer, you may encourage vigorous growth, much like spring pruning. Prune too late in the summer and new growth is vulnerable to early hard frosts and winter's deep freezes. Pruning in early June may feel more like summer in most parts of the country, but early June pruning will give rise to growth much like dormant, spring pruning.

Unfortunately for the pruner, no two seasons are alike. Often, the weather won't let you have ideal control over summer pruning. In the rainless summer areas of the West, you can expect a noticeable decline of new growth by late June. (If you water too much, you'll provoke plenty of growth.) However, in an arid climate like central California, new growth can continue at a rampant pace well into late June during a mild summer. Estimating is difficult because the same California garden might get a heat wave in May that slows new growth before June. In contrast to early-season heat, the warm, rainy summers of the Midwest can maintain active growth until fall. For ideal summer pruning, the more the new growth has naturally slowed down due to the weather and reduced water, the more control you'll achieve from pruning.

To safely remove unwanted growth, the later in the summer you prune, the better. In mild-winter areas along the California coast, this might be from early August (up North) to early September (down South). Mid August may be the last safe time for the middle of the eastern seaboard, depending on how soon the early frosts are expected to arrive. If you're unsure, ask local gardeners or the Cooperative Extension Service for frost dates. (Some trees, such as sweet cherry trees, stop growing after the year's longest day [June 21] in response to longer nights.

SUMMER PRUNING TO AVOID DISEASE

Certain plants have seasons when they are particularly prone to diseases entering a wound or pruning cut. One example is cytospora canker disease (also called perennial canker). It can enter pruning cuts made in late winter on almond, apple, cherry, nectarine, peach, pear, plum, maple, poplar, spruce, and willow trees. It is better to prune these trees in late spring or summer.

Bacterial gummosis (*Pseudomonas syringae*) attacks all stone fruit trees, lilac bushes, ornamental and edible mulberry trees, and olive trees. Bacterial canker (*P. morsprunorum*) infects all stone fruit trees, pear trees, apple trees (sometimes), citrus trees, lilac shrubs, and numerous woody plants. These two prominent diseases can also enter through pruning wounds, especially those made in late winter through early summer when it rains. Summer pruning will help avoid these troublesome diseases—*especially* in dry summer climates where they're even less potent.

Powdery mildew infects apple, pear, and plum trees, and rosebushes. If this disease is a problem in your area, avoid spring pruning altogether. Wait until summer or late summer when spring growth slows down. By not forcing succulent growth with spring pruning, this disease may have a harder time getting a foothold. (The use of fungicides is much more effective than pruning in controlling mildew.)

Another opportunistic disease, bacterial blight, often attacks cherry trees. By pruning after the crop is harvested and using a spray of copper sulfate before bloom, this disease has a chance of being controlled.

Any pruning after this time won't generate new shoots or laterals.)

Controlling the size of a tree or shrub usually requires summer pruning because more than one pruning is necessary to keep a tree or shrub in bounds. When trying to restrain a vigorous tree or shrub, pruning can be done in winter, spring, and summer. Judicious pruning all season long is best for reducing the size of overgrown trees and shrubs. However, as you become more familiar with the plants in your yard and garden, the correct amount of pruning will become more apparent. As with all pruning, watch the various growth cycles of your plants over a season or two, and pruning them will become a more instinctive process.

FALL PRUNING OF HERBACEOUS PERENNIALS

In most places, the onset of fall's diaphanous frosts and harsh freezes makes it too chancy to prune woody plants, shrubs, vines, or trees. It is, however, a fine time to tidy up the perennial flower border. Herbaceous perennials are different from trees and shrubs because most die back to the ground in the fall and return the following spring by using the food energy stored in the roots. If left uncut, herbaceous perennials can form a brown-on-brown jumble of spent foliage. This shabby heap of dead plant parts can be cut away, heaped into a compost pile, and replaced with a deep, attractive winter mulch. Some gardeners apply a more natural touch and allow the remaining spent foliage and flower heads to collect snow as a form of winter mulch. If there is little wind, the garden becomes a collection of snowy sculptures.

WINTER PRUNING

The most dangerous time to prune in cold climates is during winter. As temperatures drop below freezing, the likelihood of damage to plant tissue increases. High winds and dry air can increase the effect of cold, and the drier the soil and the plant's tissue, the more sensitive the plant is to cold. Exposed fresh pruning cuts make the plant's tissue more vulnerable to severe cold damage.

Plants differ considerably in their tolerance of cold weather. Deep into cold-winter weather, for example, it's best to leave a Japanese maple unpruned, maybe even cover it with an insulating wrap when temperatures drop below −20°F. Fig trees are an example of a frost-sensitive, nearly subtropical plant that even unpruned may have branches freeze back at only 15°F. (Fig trees will die back to their roots at 0°F, but they usually resprout in the spring.)

In moderate-winter climates, the pruning rules are completely different. Where the danger of a hard or damaging frost is rare, pruning can be done in the middle of winter. It's common for some commercial fruit orchards in California's central valley, where winters are mild, to complete all pruning by Thanksgiving or the end of December.

"SELF-PRUNING" PERENNIALS, SHRUBS, AND TREES

Bamboo, Heavenly
   (*Nandina domestica*)

Barberry, Japanese
   (*Berberis thunbergii*)

Basket-of-gold (*Aurinia saxatilis*)

**Bergenia, winter-blooming or
leather** (*Bergenia crassifolia*)

Big tree, Giant sequoia*
   (*Sequoiadendron giganteum*)

Catalpa (*Catalpa bignonioides*)

Chamomile (*Anthemis nobilis*)

Chestnut, Chinese
   (*Castanea mollissima*)

Chestnut, Horse
   (*Aesculus hippocastanum*)

Coneflower, purple
   (*Echinacea purpurea*)

Daylilies (*Hemerocallis* spp.)

Dogwood (*Cornus florida*)

Harry Lauder's Walking Stick
   (*Corylus avellana* 'Contorta')

Hellebores, Christmas rose
   (*Helleborus* spp.)

Holly, English (*Ilex aquifolium*)

Irises (*Iris* spp.)

Juniper, Creeping
   (*Juniperus horizontalis*)

Little-leaf linden* (*Tilia cordata*)

Manzanitas (*Arctostaphylos* spp.)

Mugho pine, Dwarf
   (*Pinus mugo* var. *mugo*)

Oak, Black, California*
   (*Quercus kelloggii*)

Oak, Blue* (*Q. douglasii*)

Oak, Cork* (*Q. suber*)

Oak, English* (*Q. robur*)

Oak, Holly (*Q. ilex*)

Oak, Live, Coast* (*Q. agrifolia*)

Oak, Pin* (*Q. palustris*)

Oak, Red (*Q. rubra*)

Oak, Scarlet* (*Q. coccinea*)

Oak, Shumard (*Q. shumardii*)

Oak, Valley, California*
   (*Q. lobata*)

Oak, White* (*Q. alba*)

Oak, White, Oregon Garry*
   (*Q. garryanna*)

Pecan (*Carya illinoinensis*)

Persimmon, Oriental or Japanese
   (*Diospyros kaki*)

Phlox, summer (*Phlox paniculata*)

Photinia, Chinese (*P. serrulata*)

Photinia, Japanese
   (*Photinia glabra*)

Pieris, Chinese (*Pieris forrestii*)

Privet, Japanese (as a tree)
   (*Ligustrum japonicum*)

Redwood, Coast*
   (*Sequoia sempervirens*)

Redwood, Dawn
   (*Metasequoia glyptostroboides*)

Rose, Rugosa (*Rosa rugosa*)

Russian olive
   (*Elaeagnus angustifolia*)

Star jasmine
   (*Trachelospermum jasminoides*)

Sweet gum, Liquidambar
   (*Liquidambar orientalis*)

*Large trees that need pruning every five to seven years to remove dead limbs and to thin the foliage on heavy limbs for safety's sake.

The Tools
of the Craft
and How
to Use Them

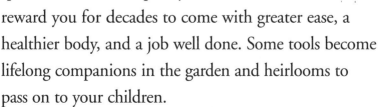

Whether you're clipping, tying, or spreading the plants in your yard, you'll need a basic set of tools; some can be simple, homemade equipment while others may be more complex, but readily purchased. When acquiring a basic set of pruning and shaping tools, don't pinch pennies (or dollars). A little more money spent on well-built, quality tools will reward you for decades to come with greater ease, a healthier body, and a job well done. Some tools become lifelong companions in the garden and heirlooms to pass on to your children.

Gardeners use their hands more than any other part of their body; and pruning is dependent on using your hands. The hand is comprised of a very complex combination of 27 bones working in conjunction with various muscles, tendons, and tissue. Older pruning tools may aggravate afflictions of the hand and wrist, but well-designed tools can help prevent these conditions or allow someone with one of these problems to continue gardening.

The advances in tool design are due to ergonomics—the study of equipment design that maximizes productivity by reducing fatigue, stress, and discomfort to the user. In other words, ergonomic equipment is designed to fit the body's shape and how it really moves and works. Just as today's car steering wheels are much fatter than the one in Henry Ford's Model T (in part, because the thicker diameter is much easier to hold and operate), the handles on most modern hand clippers are much thicker than on older models.

BASIC TOOLS

The majority of your pruning will be done with only a few tools. Generally, gardeners get the most use out of their clippers, loppers, and folding handsaw. The comfort and quality of your basic set of tools cannot be stressed enough; these tools, especially clippers, are indispensable in the garden and should therefore not hinder you in any way.

HAND CLIPPERS: All plants start out small, so a hand clipper, shear, or pruner comes in handy. This tool will be your mainstay for most pruning jobs—forever. Spare no expense to get the best hand clipper for your needs, your hands, and your plants. There are two worthwhile choices: bypass clippers and bypass clippers with a rotating handle.

BYPASS CLIPPERS: The most common design of pruners, shears, or clippers is called a bypass because the cutting edge at the end of one handle passes by the anvil on the other handle. (Another name is the hook-and-blade pruning tool.) The anvil firmly holds the shoot, lateral, or branch in place while the blade cuts. The usual bypass clipper can cut branches up to 1" in

The best hand clippers are designed to minimize strain on the hand and wrist. These have a rotating grip for less stress.

diameter—depending on whether the plant is fresh or dry, and on the strength of the pruner.

The best hand clipper should have handles curved to fit your hand. The slightly concave curve to one handle and the peculiar bend in the other handle make the pruner look odd, yet your comfort is greatly enhanced by the ergonomic design.

Consider the natural shape and positioning of your hand when looking at an old pair of pruners. The bottom handle (the gripping handle) will be either straight or curved in a way that is exactly the *opposite* of the arch made naturally by your fingers and hand. The old-fashioned, arbitrary design forces needless friction between the shears and your fingers. The first thing you'll probably notice after using an old pair of clippers are your blisters. Pruners designed with ergonomics—and your comfort—in mind, have a gripping handle with a curve to match your hand's natural shape, so they are simple, and effective—and you'll probably have fewer blisters.

The top handle (the balancing, or thumb, handle) on old pruners is straight or slightly curved. Every time you "lean into" a pruning cut, the thumb has a tendency to slip forward off the shears, thereby losing some grip and control. On the superior modern clipper, there is an odd-looking, yet effective, crook in the handle. This noticeable jog in the handle is an excellent resting place for the curve where the thumb meets the hand. The curved design prevents your hand from sliding forward off the shears, and you won't develop habits to resist this tendency.

Handles made of lightweight metal alloy reduce the overall weight of your clippers, causing you less physical toll when pruning for long periods of time. Always compare the weight of various pruners; less weight means less effort and stress on your hand. Often, the handles are made of a forged alloy different from the cutting blade and the steel in the anvil, which is sturdy enough to take any amount of abuse.

For a clean, crisp cut, a high-quality cutting blade is required. Modern technology virtually insures that the top brand-name clippers have well-forged steel. A good blade must take and hold a sharp edge. Older metal blades had softer steel that was easy to sharpen, but quick to dull. Modern blades are strong and less likely to chip or shatter, can be quickly sharpened, and hold a sharp edge for a reasonable amount of time.

The best clippers have a cutting blade slanted slightly forward to prevent your wrist from twisting towards the cut. The old-fashioned pruner's handles and blade form a straight line that forces you to rotate your wrist forward to get a good clasp on the branch every time you lean into a plant to prune. The little twist of the wrist adds up to plenty of stress with each pruning session.

Good clippers have a small channel to collect sap and resin and help divert them away from the blade. When purchasing clippers, look for this small channel along one side of the anvil. The little groove may seem insignificant, but it helps keep the blade from getting "gummed-up" with the substances. Certain plants, like fig trees, *Euphorbia* spp., and oleander shrubs, have sticky sap that causes the blade to get stuck to the anvil.

BYPASS CLIPPERS WITH A ROTATING HANDLE: When you close your fingers to make a fist, the fingers actually curl forward. But with most pruners, the handle is *fixed*, not movable, so they don't mimic the natural action of the hand—thus the invention of pruning shears with a rotating handle for extra comfort. The handle moves with your fingers, requiring 30 percent less effort to squeeze the handles. This style of clipper is perfect for gardeners with carpal tunnel syndrome symptoms, weak hands, weak wrists, or arthritis. If you are doing many hours of pruning at one time, there's the added bonus of fewer blisters.

MAINTAINING CLIPPERS

Some clippers with forged-alloy handles will form an odd-looking white crystalline growth from chlorine on the metal, if you have used a 10% bleach-and-water solution to disinfect the blade and prevent the spread of fire blight. To prevent this chemical reaction, at the end of each pruning session, simply rinse the shears in tap water, towel dry, and lightly oil. Some arborists prefer a 100% solution of Lysol™, which doesn't harm the tools. You can also use 100% rubbing alcohol.

LOPPERS: A good pair of loppers is essential for the well-tooled pruner. Some people do all of their tree pruning with a lopper, which can cut branches up to 2" in diameter—depending on the model, the length of the handles, and the strength of your wrists and arms. Some of the ergonomic improvements integrated into hand clippers can be found in modern loppers, such as lightweight metal alloy or fiberglass handles. (Wood-handle loppers are not recommended; the wood can break and the replacement handle is very difficult to install.) Again, most respected brand names have a high-quality, high-carbon steel cutting blade and narrow anvil, for easy access to narrow-angled forks between shoots, laterals, or branches. Heavy-duty, replaceable Neoprene™ rubber bumpers (shock absorbers) on both handles will protect your knuckles and wrists when cutting thick branches or limbs. Be sure to look for the little effort-saving sap channel along the anvil, and make sure you can readily purchase replacement parts.

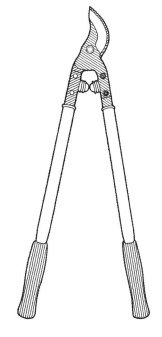

Loppers will cut thicker branches than clippers. Their long handles let you reach into the middle of bushes.

Many gardeners choose a pair of loppers with long handles with the idea that they'll get more leverage, but often the additional leverage is wasted because the 2"-diameter branches or limbs are too tough to cut. (If you routinely cut 2"-diameter branches or limbs, you're doing something wrong—unless you are restoring an abandoned tree. A tree under your seasonal care should seldom need large-diameter branches or limbs removed because it would have been done when the shoot or lateral was much smaller.)

When scrambling around the canopy of a large shrub or a tree, it's not always easy to fully open the long-handled loppers to get maximum leverage; there are too many branches in the way. Watch local professional orchard pruners and you'll notice that more pruners have switched to shorter-handle loppers, usually 15"–21" long.

PRUNING SAWS: A simple pruning saw with a 7"–12" blade is all that's necessary for the majority of your sawing needs. Some pruning saws come with fixed blades, which may or may not come with a protective sheath, while others have blades that fold into the handle when not in use. Both styles work fine when it comes to cutting, but some gardeners find the folding saws easier to use in crowded situations, like dense shrubbery or up in a tree. The folded saw can comfortably fit into a deep gardening-pant's pocket or the large pocket of old-fashioned denim overalls, or be tucked into the top of a high gardening rain boot.

If you're purchasing a folding saw, be sure it has an easy-to-use clasp to keep it open, or the saw blade could unexpectedly close on your hand. A saw blade with many teeth per inch will make a more refined, smoother cut, but requires more effort than a saw with fewer teeth per inch. For most pruning tasks, a faster cut is more important to conserve

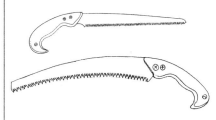

your energy for other gardening tasks. Regardless of whether you prefer a folding or rigid style, a saw is only as good as its steel. The tempered blade should be high-carbon steel and may have chrome plating. The steel used in saws is often more brittle than the steel

Pruning saws are narrow enough to fit in tight spaces between branches.

used in clipper construction. If the blade gets stuck while pruning and bows too much, the steel will snap—usually near the tip. This is why it's always wise to wear goggles or at least shatterproof glasses or sunglasses (see page 49). Many pruning saw blades hold a very sharp edge and should only be sharpened by a professional.

Unlike a carpenter's handsaw, all pruning saws cut only when *pulled* toward the pruner. Pruning saws do not cut on the push away from the gardener. This method takes some adjustment, but it's important for beginning pruners to learn.

POLE PRUNER: Pole pruners are used to clip off young shoots from the exterior of the tree's canopy. The difficulty of using this tool is caused by the awkward nooks and crannies on the inside of a tree. The blade and saw of a pole pruner are much more difficult to maneuver into a tight spot than using a ladder and clipping with a lopper or trimming with a handsaw. Professional orchard pruning crews rarely use pole pruners; they understand the ladder-and-lopper combination gives them more control, less hassle, and better speed, and is much less tiring. Tree services use pole pruners, but their clippers are often pneumatically activated to reduce stress on the user.

The most important feature to consider if you invest in a pole pruner is the pruning head. The heads are constructed of sheet, drop-forged, or die-cast metal; the smart choice is either drop-forged or die-cast metal. A pruning head made of cheap sheet metal will not stand up to ordinary wear and tear.

Most pole pruners have a rope that activates the cutting action when pulled. Do not waste your money on models that feature

Pole pruners allow you to prune young growth on small trees without a ladder.

rope all the way to, and through, the hinged or compound action blade. Invest in a head with a chain—resembling a bicycle chain—that "drives" the hinged or compound cutting action. (A good quality rope is still required to get to the chain.)

Pole pruners usually have two sliding lengths of fiberglass poles that extend from 6'–12' or 7'–14'. Pick the one that matches the height of your trees, with or without a ladder. Fiberglass handles are 2½ times lighter than wooden handles, so the prudent choice is fiberglass.

LADDER: The best ladder for pruning is a special construction that features a two-legged step section and one swinging leg to make a tripod. It's called an orchard ladder because of its prolific use in pruning and harvesting commercial orchards. The best versions are made of aluminum (they're easier to carry than heavier wooden ones) and come in heights of 6', 8', 10', 12', 14', and 16'.

Always place the steps with the two legs downhill from where you'll be working. Swing the third leg uphill and beyond where your feet will be and firmly anchor the third leg in the flat or uphill soil or turf. The wider the spread between the step section and the third leg, the sturdier the ladder will be. As a rule with all ladders, never stand on the top step or platform and keep both your feet at least one rung down from the top.

EXTRA TOOLS FOR SPECIAL JOBS

Once you're comfortable with the basic pruning tools, you can add more specialized pruning gadgets to your toolshed. As you become more adept at pruning, your arsenal of tools will grow. From the simple toothpick to the dangerous chainsaw, these tools will benefit you only if you have the proper respect and forethought to use them correctly. A large handsaw or chainsaw can do permanent damage to trees, shrubs, and you. Take the right safety precautions when using larger, mechanized tools and your pruning experience will be positive and rewarding.

LARGE HANDSAW: For big jobs, like restoring abandoned trees, a large handsaw is necessary. Large pruning saws have much sturdier steel than the small folding variety and come only with fixed blades. Most have curved or bowed blades and 4½–8 teeth per inch. The combination of a long blade with fewer teeth per inch and a deep space between teeth will result in faster cuts. With thick sap or where a fine cut is not required, choose a model with fewer number of teeth per inch and be sure to buy a saw with a built-in full handgrip.

CHAINSAWS: If you live in a forest or have mature trees, a chainsaw may be helpful, but first consider hiring out all chainsaw work. There is no faster way to do bodily harm in a yard than with a chainsaw. Make sure the person you hire has health insurance and business insurance or bonding. A reputable arborist or tree service are the best bets.

If you still want a chainsaw, buy one with the shortest bar length that you'll require. The longer the bar, the heavier the saw, and as a result, there is more weight to increase back strain. The best saws for most home use are extremely lightweight and can be operated with one hand if necessary, but they're much safer when using both hands. Hold the saw in the showroom and feel for its center of gravity; be sure the center of gravity is near your hand and that the saw's weight is balanced in your hand. Make sure the saw has anti-kickback features to protect your body and face from the blade. Sound reduction has finally become a sales feature, so be sure to compare the rated operating decibels of various models.

New models of easy-handling chain saws are lightweight, have short blades, and anti-kickback safety features.

When handling heavy machinery, it's important to purchase a full set of safety devices. Buy a complete set of headgear: hard hat, full-face screen guard, ear mufflers, and earplugs. For the ultimate safety, get a pair of Kevlar™ chaps to protect your legs from a slipped, running chainsaw. The Kevlar™ chaps can actually block a running chain from cutting through the material long enough for you to turn the saw off. Don't forget a pair of heavyweight leather work boots with steel-covered toes.

Hedge Clippers: A simple hedge or a complex topiary requires seasonal trimming with a hedge clipper. Manual hedge shears are simple to maintain, quiet, and inexpensive. Try out a pair of manual hedge shears before purchasing powered hedge shears.

The most important feature to look for in manual hedge shears is good balance. Make sure the weight at the tip doesn't put too much stress on your wrists. Short handles may be much more comfortable, while curved handles can be easier on your arms and wrists. Purchase a lightweight model to reduce strain—look for aluminum or fiberglass handles. Like loppers, make sure there are one or two rubber shock absorbers (bumpers) to protect your wrists.

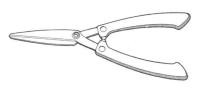

Pruning a large, unruly hedge is a daunting task for any gardener and good steel blades are essential. Hedge clippers come in a range of blade styles: some have two straight blades and others feature one or two

Look for hedge clippers that are lightweight and have top-quality steel blades.

blades that are wavy or serrated. Wavy edges means they'll probably need to be sharpened professionally, but they can easily grab hold of shoots.

Straight blades are best for more delicate foliage or more frequent trimming as they do less damage, if carefully used.

Electric and gas-powered hedgers are for big pruning jobs. The gas-powered models make more noise than the electric version, but their range of mobility is unlimited. Electric hedgers are limited to the length of the extension cord you buy—larger gauge wire (more costly) can reach farther than small gauge wire. (BEWARE: The big danger with electric hedgers is cutting the extension cord and being electrocuted. Proceed cautiously.) Be sure to get the lightest model, whether you choose gas or electric hedgers, with the weight balanced close to your

Powered hedgers are very helpful when pruning large or long hedges. Be sure to hold the cord away from the cutting bar.

hand. Either version should have a dual-reciprocating blade that cuts shoots and laterals up to ¾" in diameter. The higher quality two-cycle gasoline models have blades that can be rotated up to 180° relative to the handle and engine. Look for the models with dual-handle controls that stop the cutting action when either handle is released.

SHARPENERS: The most satisfactory sharpening tool is one that's easy to use wherever pruning takes you. Sharpening a pruning tool at the workbench or potting table is easy and relatively conventional, but sharpening a tool 20' off the ground in an oak tree can be a harrowing, if not dangerous, experience.

Metal files are good for putting the initial edge on a tool at the beginning of the pruning season, occasionally during the year, or before each pruning session. Make sure the file is held at a slight angle to the blade and file down enough metal to match the width and angle of the blade's cutting edge. A metal file with a solid wooden handle is best for easy, steady sharpening. Long metal files are rather awkward to carry up in a tree, but similar to a folding saw, they can be carried in a back pocket, in high rain boots, or in the tool pocket on the right leg of a pair of overalls. A metal file can take a lot of metal off a steel blade, so use it with discretion.

The best sharpening tool for convenient and repeated use anywhere in the garden is a metal rod embedded with diamond dust. After a metal file has put a good edge on the blade, this tool can add to the cutting edge's sharpness. Some models come with a handle that quickly unscrews and converts to a carrying case or folds shut. Some diamond sharpeners come with a leather pouch that attaches to your belt next to the pouch for the clippers.

Various forms of sharpening stones—triangular, flat, long, and squat—can put a finer edge on a blade. Some are used dry and others are used wet or with oil, but all sharpening stones are more fragile than metal files or sharpening rods. Since sharpening stones are not conveniently mobile, it's best to use them only in a shed or at a workbench.

WIDE-BRIMMED HAT, AND SUNGLASSES OR SCREENED GOGGLES: A hat and sunglasses or screened goggles are essential to protect your eyes from serious injury. Many trees have thorns or spurs that can quickly inflict serious damage on your eyes. A wide-brimmed straw hat may warn you—as you move or turn your head—of an incoming spur or thorn that brushes against your hat, making a noticeable sound. You'll be amazed how rapidly your neck will reflexively jerk away from the intruding spur or thorn.

Even if you don't react quickly enough, sunglasses, even on a dark and cloudy day, will give your eyes an extra measure of protection. Sunglasses are a good precaution, but they still have open sides that are vulnerable to a puncturing shoot, lateral, or thorn. Screen- or wire-mesh goggles are the very best in eye protection. There are many types of plastic goggles, but they quickly fog up—especially on a cold day. Screen-covered goggles let

When pruning, wear wire-mesh goggles to keep from getting poked in the eye by an errant branch. If outdoors for any length of time, add a wide-brimmed hat and sunscreen to prevent sunburn.

sweat out but are impenetrable to all but the finest sawdust. A quality pair of goggles is a must for the safety-conscious pruner.

TOOLS FOR SHAPING: Most of the tools necessary for shaping are deceptively simple. The impact of some carefully placed toothpicks or clothespins on the final shape of a mature shrub or tree is astounding.

Common toothpicks are extremely effective for spreading a new, supple shoot to a wider angle by midsummer. The best toothpicks are round, not flat, solid wood with a point on both ends.

Clothespins are used to spread slightly older growth in midsummer or to bend the tip of a 12"–18" new shoot into an arch so it becomes more fruitful. The only clothespins that work for training trees are the classic wooden variety with the spring clip. They are available in bags of 50 and they can be reused forever.

Fishing sinkers of various sizes are ideal to weigh down misbehaving one- or two-year-old shoots or laterals. Sinkers come in many weights and sizes; buy a range of them, from several ounces to nearly a pound. Fishing line works well to secure the sinkers to older branches.

For growth that's two or more years old, you'll need a sturdy spreader to hold stubborn limbs to a wider angle. You can make your own spreader sticks by putting nail points in 1½" square stakes of various lengths or by notching lath boards with a V at each end (see page 66).

The Methods *of* Pruning

Pruning is not simply cutting away at a tree or a shrub. For every desired growth pattern, there is a specific pruning method. Become more familiar with the various techniques, and your success as a pruner will be reflected in your plants. In many instances, your hand tool and your mind are all you need. When it comes to making cuts, proceeding with abandon is almost never the prudent approach. Knowing how to make different types of cuts—along with understanding why you're cutting and what the desired result will be—is the final piece of the pruning puzzle.

Simple Techniques

Pinching and rubbing off buds are the easiest forms of pruning. Simple thinning and heading cuts—made with regard to bud placement—are the most common types of pruning practiced by the home gardener. Notching and ringing are advanced methods to be practiced with caution. If you start with the basics and proceed cautiously to more difficult cuts, like removing a mature branch, your pruning experience will be fruitful and you'll quickly find yourself arching branches to get the most bloom and disbudding roses to produce wonderfully large flowers.

Pinching Back: Pinching back is the simple removal of a tip bud—and thus its dominance over lower dormant buds—that often invigorates a number of shoots. Pinching back a shoot is a common way to stimulate one or more side shoots. This way, herbaceous plants, such as fuchsias, chrysanthemums, pelargoniums, poinsettias, and coleuses, are made to have fuller, more dense, foliage and better subsequent bloom. A regular part of seasonal pruning with many herbaceous perennials involves pinching back with your fingernails, clippers, or shears. Since pinching back is used to stimulate leafy shoots, which then make flower buds, the spring prior to bloom is reserved for stimulating shoots and shaping. Stop pinching back before flower buds begin to show. Pinch back woody shrubs to a well-placed dormant bud or set of opposing buds on each stem. If the shoot is too tough, use clippers.

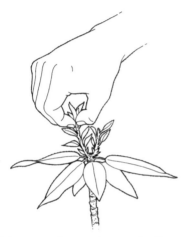

Using your fingernails to pinch off a soft stem tip is an easy way to stimulate branching and wider growth habit.

Shearing: Shearing is nonselective pinching back of numerous tip buds that often doubles the number of side shoots. You can shear a plant's tip buds with hand-held bypass clippers, hand hedge clippers, or mechanical hedge clippers. Using a bypass clipper is faster than pinching back but still more time-consuming than using hedge clippers. Both types of hedge clippers, however, can leave the foliage slightly coarse; they're best reserved for herbaceous perennials with tight foliage, shrubs with small leaves, or any plant that quickly fills in its foliage after shearing. (Pinching back takes more time but leaves the foliage looking fresh and less ragged than when hedge clippers are used.)

DISBUDDING/RUBBING: Disbudding is simply done by rubbing the unwanted buds off with a finger or thumb. Rose growers (or professional rosarians) trying to cultivate the largest, most gorgeous blooms for competition will often disbud to promote size. Any plant that makes flower buds can be disbudded to enlarge the remaining flowers. Start rubbing off buds as soon as you spot the young flower buds. The difficulty with disbudding is that many plants make so many flower buds that it can be a very tedious process.

DEADHEADING: Removing spent blossoms from any plant is called deadheading. To deadhead, pinch off individual flower stalks, clip one or more spent flower heads with a hand clipper, or shear all the blossom stems using manual or powered hedge clippers. Many herbaceous perennials look better with a shearing after flowering. Deadheading tends to be a very personal topic; fastidious gardeners carefully remove the dead blooms from just about every plant, while gardeners who champion the natural look shy away from deadheading.

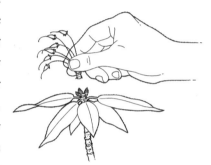

Removing old flower heads, a process called deadheading, makes a plant look neat and can encourage better growth.

THE ANATOMY OF A PROPER CUT

The most important aspects of any cut are location and angle; the right mix of both is important to maintaining the health of your tree or shrub and encouraging growth where you want it. Whether you're cutting next to dormant buds or removing large branches, it's smart to take your time and be sure that your pruning does not damage the plant or invite rot and disease.

CORRECT CUTS NEXT TO DORMANT BUDS: When cutting back to a dormant bud, don't cut too close or too far away from the bud. The proper cut leaves a tiny portion of the shoot—no longer than ¼"—

above the bud. The cut should be made at a slight angle to the stem, parallel to the angle of the bud. But make sure the lower angle of the cut is not below the bud on the back side of the shoot. The slightly angled cut

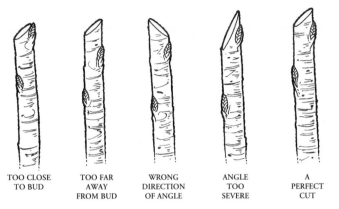

| TOO CLOSE TO BUD | TOO FAR AWAY FROM BUD | WRONG DIRECTION OF ANGLE | ANGLE TOO SEVERE | A PERFECT CUT |

A pruning cut must be correctly angled at 45° away from the bud, leaving ¼" of stem. Cutting at the wrong angle or leaving too much stem invites rot.

is easier than cutting perpendicular to the shoot and is less likely to crush it. Also the diagonal cut may dry off faster after rains or irrigation.

CLIP FOR DIRECTION: One of the most important details in pruning is the direction of dormant buds next to pruning cuts. Every bud, located randomly around the stem, is already pointed in a certain direction. Pruning cuts on one-, two-, or three-year-old growth are made next to a shoot, a lateral, or a dormant bud, but the choice of where to cut is dictated by the shape of the scaffold and the location of the first bud below the proposed cut. The bud below the cut could easily grow in the wrong direction for the scaffold shape the following season, even though the shoot growth length looks good.

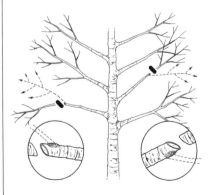

To direct growth, cut a branch back to a side shoot or a bud growing in the direction where growth is desired.

Always cut back to a dormant bud that faces the proper direction for the desired growth. While pruning, pay attention to the direction of every bud in the vicinity of your cut. If you want your tree or shrub to grow vertically, the buds should be on the top side of the shoot. If you want the tree or shrub to be more wide than tall, choose only buds facing outward or buds on the bottom section of the stem.

IDENTIFY THE BRANCH COLLAR: The safest way to prune requires the pruner to identify two parts of the limb attachment: the branch collar and the branch bark ridge (see page 11). The branch collar often looks like a slightly swollen or shoulder-shaped lump at the base of a shoot, branch, or limb. (Conifers usually have a prominent branch collar.) If the plant doesn't have an easily recognized branch collar, you can use the branch bark ridge to figure out the best cut.

If you can't spot the branch collar, don't guess by leaving a long stubby piece of the shoot, lateral, or branch. The stub can be colonized by diseases and fungi that may subsequently enter the heart of the branch or trunk.

CUT BIG BRANCHES IN THREE STEPS: To cut branches bigger than 2" in diameter, special care needs to be taken so the tree is not harmed. Larger branches should not be removed with one cut; the branch's weight will tear it off the tree before you're finished cutting, and a wide, long strip of bark may be torn off the trunk beneath the branch. When this happens, a larger section of the tree's interior is exposed to disease and rot.

The safest way to prune larger branches is done by making three cuts. The first cut should be made at least 1' away from the trunk on the branch's underside. Cut upward one-quarter to one-third of the way through the branch. Next, cut the top of the branch 2"

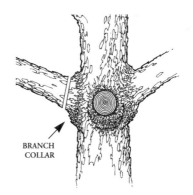

BRANCH
COLLAR

Avoid flush cuts (see above) that remove protective branch collars. When cutting off tree limbs, angle the final cut outside the collar to prevent disease.

or less outward from the first cut until the branch snaps off. The first underside cut will stop any ripping bark. The final cut is made near the top of the branch bark ridge, leaving the branch collar intact.

REMOVING SUCKERS: All true root suckers should be removed each summer. One sure way to accomplish this is by digging down to

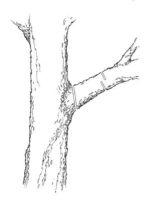

the roots and trimming the suckers off as you would prune a shoot, leaving the stem's collar intact. Another method, which should be done in midsummer after the sucker's growth has begun to stiffen just a little, is to wrap the whiplike growth tightly around one hand and, yanking with all your might, separate the base of the sucker from the rootstock. This tactic may seem brutal, but any lighter treatment will favor the regrowth of the sucker. (Never clip the suckers off at the soil's surface.

When removing large branches, first remove the bulk of the branch, leaving a foot-long stub. Cut upward partway through the branch, and then cut downward outside the first cut. Lastly, trim off the stub outside the branch collar.

If you do, the shoot from the surface down to the base of the sucker has plenty of dormant buds waiting to sprout with the removal of the tip bud's stifling hormone.)

HOW TO CUT

There is a complete repertoire of pruning cuts at your disposal, but there are only two basic cuts: heading cuts and thinning cuts. Heading cuts remove part of a branch, limb, or shoot. Done to stimulate growth, heading cuts remove growth back to a bud. Thinning cuts remove an entire branch, limb, or shoot back to its origin. These cuts are made to control growth or shape the overall plant.

Determine which cut is the best for your particular need (or plant) and pay close attention to the results. Remember, much of pruning is about observation; follow your plant's lead and the right cut will become more obvious. Always bear in mind what growth, or lack thereof, will result from your pruning cuts and you're well on your way to clipping with confidence.

HEADING CUTS: In general, a heading cut (also called heading back) is the partial removal of a branch. To an arborist, a heading cut removes growth back to an existing lateral, branch, or limb that isn't big enough or isn't in position to assume the role of a primary branch in the canopy, but will improve the overall form. In reference to fruit trees, heading also means cutting back a one-year-old shoot to one of the dormant buds (not to the base of the current or previous year's growth) to provoke one or more side shoots.

Heading cuts made in the spring (especially during the dormant season) encourage sprouting near the cut end. The extra shoots that are stimulated may help fill in the scaffold—especially when heading back to dormant buds on shoots. One drawback to heading dormant buds, however, is that the new growth tends to be crowded and upright with a narrow angle of attachment. (Use thinning cuts [see page 58] the following summer to remove a number of the shoots, which will usually allow for more lateral branching.)

Heading back to an existing shoot, lateral, or branch will often help divert the sap flow and provoke fewer new shoots compared with cutting back to a dormant or trace bud. If you want to limit growth, head back long, horizontal shoots; it will not stimulate as much new growth as a more severe pruning or cutting of vertical shoots, laterals, or branches.

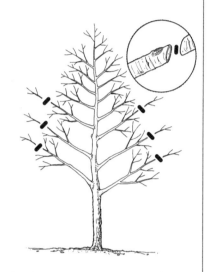

A heading cut removes a portion of a stem or shoot, often leaving a properly placed dormant bud behind.

All conifers can be "headed back" to make them fuller, by lightly pruning their "candles."

TOPPING

An outdated approach to pruning more familiar to arborists than orchardists, topping is the removal of the upper portion of a leader. More specifically, topping is like heading back to any lateral growth that isn't big enough to resume the role of a terminal shoot. If the remaining shoot is less than one-half of the diameter that was removed, it's considered topping. Many gardeners and arborists used to cut out all of the top, or vertical, growth of trees to control their height, resulting in flat, wide tops. Unfortunately, topped trees die much sooner due to rot and disease entering the exposed leaders, limbs, and branches.

Trees that require topping are poorly placed trees; the wrong tree for the place. Examples include tall pines planted beneath utility wires, large oaks planted beneath the eaves of a house, or tall vertical trees planted along a fence—in the way of a scenic view. This technique must be abandoned. Instead, selective thinning over a number of years will control the tree's height before it gets too tall. Better yet, take the poorly chosen tree out, plant it in a more suitable spot, and replant the area with a tree or shrub with the proper mature size for the spot.

Avoid heading cuts on mature trees; the effect is similar to the debilitating impact of topping. Heading cuts made on full-grown central leader trees will open up the tree to pests, rots, and diseases.

THINNING CUTS: A thinning cut (also called thinning out) is the complete removal of a lateral by cutting it back to the base of its growth. The origin of growth is often another lateral big enough to become the new, or replacement, leader. (Remember, laterals are not just horizontal shoots, but any shoot growing at any angle from older growth.) Gardeners often use "thinning cut" to refer to cutting any age growth back to its base. Since thinning cuts may produce fewer shoots than heading cuts, they are best used to remove watersprouts. Thinning cuts are most effective at controlling vertical growth and reducing the crown of a tree or shrub while retaining its overall scaffold shape. A thinning cut can be made during any season; however, to reduce resprouting, it's best to thin well after the spring flush of growth during peak summer pruning.

To thin, merely cut the entire shoot or lateral off at the shoulder-like branch collar. On current season's growth, the branch collar may be unobtrusive, but it is readily displayed on older growth. Remember, cutting in the spring or summer gives the callus time to begin forming while the plant is actively photosynthesizing, which helps the callus cover the cut more quickly. (Callusing covers spring pruning cuts by three to six times more area than summer cuts because of the extra growing time.)

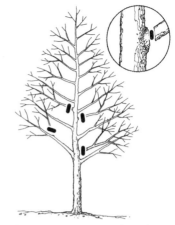

A thinning cut removes a branch or stem at its origin.

THE DANGER OF FLUSH CUTS: The goal of pruning is to remove unwanted growth *without* causing rot at the heart of the stem,

shoot, branch, limb, or trunk. Cutting flush to the trunk, lateral, or shoot actually leaves the plant more vulnerable to rot. Under no circumstances should you cut a branch flat to the trunk.

Until recently, most gardening books endorsed the old adage that each pruning cut should be made flush with the trunk, limb, or branch. Flush cuts actually harm plants by cutting away part of the protective zone of cells in the branch collar. The modern approach to pruning takes a little more skill but leaves the entire protective zone intact.

Flush cuts are particularly destructive because woody plants have special plant tissues that protect the inner wood (the trunk or

CALLUS FORMATION

A callus is undifferentiated tissue formed by the cambium layer around a wound or pruning cut. Noticeable as a swollen lump of tissue from the live bark that grows around the cut surface, a callus forms as a result of numerous changes in the tissue surrounding the wound or cut.

You can easily tell if old pruning cuts were properly made. A healthy, mature callus forms completely around the wound of the cut. After one or more years, depending on the size of the cut, a flush cut or improperly made cut often produces only an oval callus that doesn't meet either at the top or bottom of the oval.

heartwood on trees) from rot. These naturally occurring tissues form specific zones (also called compartments) made of rot-resistant cell walls. Any rot-promoting fungi or microorganisms that try to enter the core of the stem, branch, or trunk are effectively cordoned-off in a process called compartmentalization. In short, flush cuts should be avoided because they compromise built-in defenses against rot.

SPECIAL MEASURES TO ENCOURAGE GROWTH

Sometimes our most earnest efforts to stimulate growth do not succeed. In such cases, more extreme pruning methods are often necessary. Notching and ringing, techniques that involve purposeful scarring to your tree, can result in new growth where you want it. Be aware though, these methods should be considered experimental by the beginning pruner, and should be practiced with extreme caution because they can put the health of your trees and shrubs at risk.

A PRUNING PIONEER

The man who first revealed the erroneous nature of flush cuts and pruning tar is Dr. Alex Shigo, a former forest pathologist with the U.S. Forest Service in New Hampshire. Shigo has done more to reshape our understanding of tree growth and pruning than any single person. He has dissected over 15,000 trees with a chainsaw to determine how injury, pathogens, and pruning affected growth, rot, and disease. One of his many studies involved planting walnut trees, pruning them in various ways, and cutting the trees open twelve years later to analyze the effects of pruning.

NOTCHING: Notching is a simple technique used by fruit growers to invigorate a flower bud or a lateral. (It also works with many ornamental trees.) Flower buds and new shoots don't always emerge precisely where you want them, but this special technique can encourage—with better odds than Nature—where a flower bud, lateral, or shoot will form. The technique got its name from using a knife to pare a wide, shallow notch into the lateral. A ¼"–⅜" round rat-tail file works much better and keeps you from gouging the lateral too deeply. This technique works best with the current season's growth or two-year-old branches with visible plump (not declining) dormant buds.

To turn a dormant bud into a flower bud, simply notch (scar) the bark halfway around the lateral *below* the bud. Carve a wide, but not deep, wound in the bark; too deep and the lateral will snap. Stroke the lateral like you would bow a violin, making sure to go at least 180° around the lateral. The technique prompts flowers because the leaf attached to the dormant bud can no longer send any food back into the tree. The extra carbohydrates build up within the bud and stimulate flower formation.

If your goal is a lateral where one hasn't grown, simply notch *above* the dormant bud. By scoring above the bud, the path of the stifling hormonal signal from the tip bud to the dormant bud is severed. Without the signal, the dormant bud thinks it's on top of the lateral and produces vegetative growth.

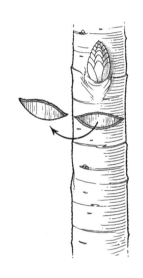

Both of these techniques are best done on current season's growth or two-year-old branches well after the rush of spring growth to prevent vigorous callusing. When notching in early spring, the vigor of the sap flow can cause a

Notching the bark below a bud on a fruit tree can turn a dormant bud into a flower bud.

callus to quickly cover the wound and negate or minimize the effect of the scoring. If the area scored, above or below a bud, were to callus over, the stifling hormone might return and the new lateral or flower would not grow at all or would grow less vigorously.

RINGING IN FLOWER AND FRUIT: Ringing is a courageous measure used for branches that refuse to flower (and, with fruit trees that refuse to bear fruit). Ringing can also be used to dwarf a tree, form flower buds, promote fruiting, increase the size of fruit, increase the fruit's sugar content, and promote earlier fruiting.

Ringing involves removing a strip of bark from around the entire circumference of a branch. Although some recommend the width of the strip to be from ⅒"–1", most pruners agree that the ring should be ¼" or less. Experiment by removing a narrower band of bark at first, then try wider rings or separate branches. The bark should slip cleanly from the sapwood in spring. Do not treat the exposed area with grafting tar or paint. Instead, cover it with surgical tape, adhesive tape, or cotton strips to help the callus cover the wound.

The aim of ringing is to remove a portion of the young bark and allow a callus to bridge the gap. One theory holds that the carbohydrates traveling down the bark are restricted and stay in the branches longer to produce more flowers and fruit.

This technique must be treated as experimental and dangerous. At first, practice only on shoots you can afford to lose.

GIRDLING

Girdling is a technique used exclusively by fruit growers. It involves cutting a wide strip of bark off of the entire circumference of the stem or trunk. Controlled partial girdling attempts to shock a nonblooming or unfruitful branch, limb, or tree into flowering. The bark is separated at the cambium layer. If the strip is wide enough so callusing doesn't span the gap, then the layers of transport to and from the roots and canopy fail to do their job and the foliage above the girdle withers and can die. This is a technique that must be used cautiously and with discretion.

METHODS *for* SHAPING

Prune is done by clipping, sawing, and lopping. The forest "prunes" using gravity and the wind. The forest also shapes itself by bending; it uses gravity, ice, snow, natural growth, and even wildlife. Bending, spreading, and weighting are practices that you can use to avoid lots of remedial pruning later in the lives of your plants. Used correctly, these shaping techniques insure the proper placement and angle of young shoots, laterals, and 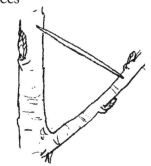 branches. And when shaping techniques are used in various combinations, you can encourage branching, bloom, and fruitfulness.

Shaping guides growth with little or no clipping or sawing. The methods for shaping are remarkably simple and economical: toothpicks or clothespins (for shaping purposes, the only clothespin suitable is the wooden "clip-on" variety with a spring) spread young shoots; fishing sinkers and other weights lower shoots, laterals, and branches; twine pulls a shoot, lateral, or branch up or down; even sticks can spread older branches; and the occasional clip with the pruning shears augments any shaping project. While there are numerous techniques and devices recommended for shaping, a creative gardener can be innovative, using a range of homemade equipment.

There are three main reasons to shape—instead of prune—ornamental and fruiting trees. First, rampant vertical growth can be slowed down easily and encouraged to produce more lateral growth by merely tying or weighting the tip bud to a lower angle, thus eliminating its dominance. Second, progressively bending a shoot down to 45°–60° will often turn dormant buds into flower buds (an especially good technique for fruit trees). Third, on fruit trees, young, vertical growth with a narrow attachment can be spread to 45°–60°. This wider-angled attachment will encourage more flower buds and allow more light into the canopy for improved fruit color and flavor.

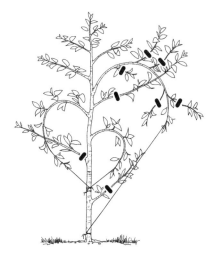

Arching young shoots on fruit and ornamental trees can make them more floriferous and productive. Fruit will form on the middle to outer third of the arch.

All shaping objectives and techniques must be adjusted to how the tree or shrub naturally grows. Genetics is a more powerful influence than pruning; if a tree or shrub typically grows with a narrow angle of attachment, then there's not much you can do to cause a 45°–60° angle. If the angle of a shoot or branch is extremely narrow, look at the branch bark ridge to see if it has a fissure or has folded in on itself. If this is the case, some of the bark tissue has grown inside the limb or branch (called included bark) and spreading won't do any good. It's best to prune off young limbs showing included bark at the branch bark ridge. This problem often happens when two vertical leaders, or codominant shoots or branches, are competing; remove one of the two as soon as you spot the problem.

ARCHING

Spur-type trees (ornamental trees and most deciduous fruit trees that flower on two-year-old branches and for years thereafter) respond quite well to arching. Bend a young shoot into an arch in the spring and it will stimulate the bud nearest the top of the arch to sprout, becoming another vertical shoot with a dominant tip bud. (This can be permanently removed with summer pruning.) More importantly, many of the buds on the outer third of the arch become flower buds, or short lateral growth, slowing the tip growth down considerably or stopping it altogether. Arching is quickly becoming recognized as an easy way to promote flower and fruit formation.

SPREADING

A brand-new shoot sometimes sprouts at a very narrow angle to its branch. A shoot with a wider angle may look more pleasing, flower better, or make more fruit. If you want a wider-angled shoot (and subsequently a wide-angled branch and limb), spread the shoot while it's still supple and malleable.

SPREADING WITH CLOTHESPINS: One clothespin can be used to force a very young shoot to a lower angle. More than one clip-on clothespin is often necessary to weigh down a slightly older shoot to the proper angle. If one clothespin doesn't lower the shoot enough, continue adding more until the ideal angle is achieved. Be careful that the clothespins are not attached too close to the end of the shoot or you'll bend the tip over and stop the subsequent lengthening. The clothespins can be removed by fall because the shoot will become more rigid and hold its position. Clothespins should be reused each year.

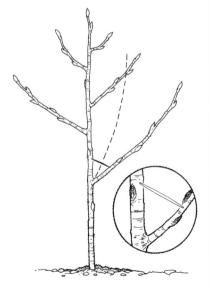

Simple household toothpicks can be used to spread young branches into desirable wide angles.

SPREADING WITH TOOTH-PICKS: By early summer, new shoots have stiffened enough so that you can use a toothpick to spread the angle of attachment. Stick one end of a wooden toothpick into the trunk's bark a few inches above where the shoot originated, bend the shoot out a little farther than the desired final angle, and stick the other end of the toothpick into any spot on the

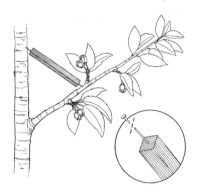

Spreading boards can be made at home. Pound nails into either end of a wooden tomato stake and clip the heads off at an angle with wire cutters.

shoot that achieves the desired angle. If the shoot is too stiff or you bend it too far, it will snap off. If the new shoot is too young and succulent, the toothpick will skewer the shoot. If this happens, wait a few weeks to try again; other shoots will have stiffened enough. If the toothpick is inserted too high on either shoot, it may fall out from lack of tension. In this case, lower one or both ends of the toothpick and it should stay in place even on a windy day. By fall, the new growth will have stiffened enough so that you can remove the toothpick; the branches (formerly young shoots) should hold most of their wider angle.

SPREADING WITH BOARDS, STRINGS, OR WEIGHTS:

Older growth—mature branches or limbs—can be spread with spreader boards, string, or weights. When growth is two or more years old, it has already begun to stiffen, so these devices will have to remain in place for

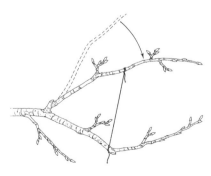

Branches can be spread into wider angles by tying them to lower branches.

two or more years, allowing the branch to toughen in the new position. When the spreading tool is taken away, the branch or limb will hold most of its new position. Spreading devices can be added at any time of the year.

There are two types of spreader boards that you can make at home. A simple lath board can be cut to various lengths from 6"–36".

(Before you cut a piece for your spreader, measure the distance between the branches where the spreader will go and cut to size.) Cut a V-notch into both ends of each piece of lath. With your new notched spreaders in hand, find a shoot, lateral, or small branch above or below the branch you want to spread and insert the spreader so the branch is growing at the desired angle.

A second type of spreader can be made from various lengths of wooden tomato stakes or ½" square wood pieces. Using six-penny, 2" *box* nails (no big head), hammer each nail half its length into each end of the sticks. Clip the small round head off each nail with a wire cutter and be sure to cut the nail head at an angle to leave a sharp point. This style of spreader is more readily installed in the tree since no corresponding lateral is required to hold it in place. To use the spreader, insert one nail point into the main trunk and bend the narrowly attached branch or limb slightly past the desired angle. Then, insert the other nail point into the branch and let the tension of the branch or limb hold the spreader in place.

For older branches, weighting is an effective technique for the often long-term process of redirecting the growth of branches that have begun to stiffen. There are no set rules for tying and weighting; it's often at the whim of the creative gardener. Twine can be used to pull a wayward branch or limb into position. One common method is to tie the young branch to an older part of the tree or to a stake in the ground. One

POORLY ANGLED BRANCHES

Occasionally, a tree will sprout a lateral that grows perpendicular to the trunk or grows toward the ground. To train the wayward branch or limb back up to a more ideal angle for flower, tip-bud, or shoot growth, simply tie a string partway out on the shoot or lateral where the growth has stiffened slightly and tie the other end higher up in the tree.

This does not apply to ornamental trees that have naturally perpendicular branches and limbs such as **Eastern redbud** (*Cercis candensis*), **American beech** (*Fagus grandiflora*), and **American plane-tree** (*Platanus occidentalis*), or cascading branches such as **Swamp oak** (*Quercus bicolor*), **Northern pin oak** (*Q. ellipsoidalis*), **Shingle oak** (*Q. imbricaria*), and **Pin oaks** (*Q. palustris*).

innovative gardener put one end of the string around a large rock, which allowed for the stone to be moved out a little at a time over several months, and thus induced a great number of flower buds. Be sure to take the string off of the branch before it starts to girdle (sink into the new bark) the branch or limb.

Any manner of heavy objects can be used to weigh down an inflexible branch or limb into position. Some people have used various-size fishing sinkers, large metal nuts looped on a string, little paper cups filled with concrete with a paper-clip hook added, and all manner of scrap metal. It's important to make sure these "objets d'art" don't blow in the wind and cause damage to the tree. Watch out for wire hooks because they will quickly be absorbed into a branch's tissue if they're not adjusted each season or removed quickly.

Plant-*by*-Plant Pruning

ROSES

Consisting of more than 100 species and 20,000 or more cultivars (named varieties), roses are a galaxy of plants. Roses (*Rosa* spp.) could rightly be included in the shrub and rambling vine sections in this book, but they're so popular they deserve special presentation.

Everybody wants to grow roses, in every climate. In Florida, roses bloom every month of the year. In Spokane, Washington, the last frost may be in May and the first in September, but there are ardent rose growers. With all the divergent climates and microclimates, no general introduction to rose pruning can do the subject justice, but luckily the fundamentals are reasonably simple. Extra help is available from the American Rose Society, which has chapters located throughout the country. Most of these horticultural organizations sponsor rose-pruning workshops each spring, and there's nothing better than seeing a hands-on demonstration. There are basic pruning guidelines for all the major groups of roses; if you follow them, you will be rewarded with a crop of blossoms sufficient to please almost any gardener.

THE WORLD OF ROSES

Broadly speaking, roses can be classified into two groups, both of which require their own type of pruning. The two groups are *everblooming* roses, which bloom on and off during the summer, and *once-blooming* roses, which produce a glorious burst of bloom once each growing season.

GRAFTED AND ROOTED ROSES

Regardless of the type of rose or its name, all roses need to have their root suckers pruned. Most commercial rose sources graft a single bud of a desired cultivar onto a rootstock. The rootstock has none of the flowering characteristics of the cultivar; it is chosen for its vigor, hardiness, and overall health. When a variety is budded onto a rootstock, any suckers have the qualities of the rootstock, not the flowering portion of the plant, so grafted rosebushes should have all suckers removed as soon as they appear. If left uncut, these suckers may overgrow the bush with flowering shoots (called *canes*), which have inferior blooms.

Some old garden roses (often referred to as old-fashioned, heirloom, or heritage roses) are grown on their "own root," from cuttings. Any suckers that form on the roots will have all the traits of the plant above ground, including the same type and quantity of bloom. However, suckers from own-rooted roses should still be removed so the shrub doesn't spread too widely or get too dense. If clipped from the root—not yanked out—these suckers will usually have roots and can be transplanted to other places in the garden.

Many roses are further classified by their growth habit. Species, or "wild" old garden roses, such as gallica, Bourbon, and hybrid perpetual roses, are once-bloomers. Shrub roses come in all different varieties and cultivars that include both once-blooming and everblooming varieties. Shrub everbloomers include floribunda, grandiflora, dwarf polyantha, and miniature roses. Finally, there are climbing roses, which are further subdivided by climbers—those with pliable canes able to cover an arbor—and ramblers, which have very tough canes and are best let to spread out over ground.

EVERBLOOMING ROSES: For obvious reasons, everblooming roses are more popular than once-blooming varieties. The everblooming group also includes modern roses such as hybrid teas, floribunda, grandiflora, miniature, and some types of old garden roses, like tea and china roses, that are adapted to warmer climates. Everblooming roses bear the best flowers and most bloom on new growth, which are the shoots produced during the current growing season. Therefore, the most effective way to enhance the flowering of everblooming roses is to encourage new growth by pruning the roses back somewhat severely in early spring, just as growth begins.

PRUNING EVERBLOOMING ROSES: Prune leafy growth sparingly as it serves to feed the roots and the whole plant so it can produce a bigger crop of new canes each season. (Large, healthy plants have more food stored in their roots, stems, and shoots to produce a greater number of bigger blossoms.) Whenever possible, encourage large plants by not pruning back too radically. (This isn't possible in cold-winter areas with temperatures regularly below 10°F, as the plants must be pruned back to 1' or less and mulched for the winter.) Conversely, unpruned roses only bear blooms at the outer edges of the plant on new growth, which gets spindly without pruning. So prune evenly to encourage new growth.

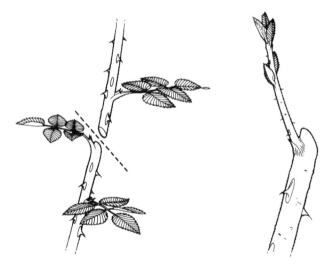

When cutting rose canes, making a slanting cut above a promising bud encourages vigorous new growth.

In mild climates, prune everblooming roses in the spring when dormant buds (called "eyes" in rosarian circles) begin to swell. In the summer, cut all canes that have flowered by one-third to one-half in length with heading cuts to an outward-facing bud (eye) or shoot. Make your cuts at a 45° angle above a healthy bud and not too close to the bud.

When clipping roses for bouquets, cut only enough stem to match the vase. This leaves as much growth as possible to feed the overall vigor of the plant. Simply cut the rose bloom and stem back to leave at least two sets of the typical five-leaflet rose leaves.

During the summer and fall, most roses will bloom longer if you remove all spent blossoms. Be sure to remove the entire flower *truss*, which is the multistemmed flower cluster, down to the first healthy bud that is growing to the outside of the bush.

HYBRID TEA ROSES: Since the introduction of the first hybrid tea rose—also called "large-flowered bush roses" because of their immense blossoms—they have become very popular. In fact, many rosarians grow

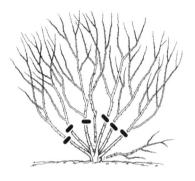

Before: During the dormant season, remove all but the strong, well-spaced canes. To protect the plant in winter climates, cut the remaining canes back to about 6" high.

After: Strong, new growth that arises from the main canes should be kept open enough for good sun and air penetration. Spent flowers can be removed at the first outward-facing shoot or bud.

these roses for exhibition in highly competitive shows. Most home gardeners clip the blooms for cut flowers, so the focus when pruning hybrid tea roses is to get as much rebloom as possible. Hybrid teas flower most heavily in two flushes—in early to midsummer and in the late summer or early fall—but they will flower regularly throughout the season until the first frost arrives.

PRUNING HYBRID TEA ROSES: Cut back new plants in early spring to 6" canes with two to four eyes each. This will stimulate vigorous canes capable of holding the large blossoms. With heading cuts, remove canes that are weak or not vertical enough to hold the weighty blooms. Prune faded flowers to sustain the period of bloom and cut back the individual flower stems to the first healthy and outward-facing shoot or eye for the next round of growth.

ONCE-BLOOMING ROSES: Once-blooming roses bear a heavy flush of flowers in late spring or early summer, and then bloom only sparingly or not at all until next year. This group includes most of the "species roses," or wild-type old garden roses such as gallica, Bourbon, and hybrid perpetual roses, which are hardy in cold-winter climates. Some of these old garden roses will rebloom to some degree after the end of their first flush of flowers fades. But the primary flush of blooms will appear in late spring or early summer on shoots that sprang forth and matured during the previous year.

PRUNING ONCE-BLOOMING (SPECIES AND OLD GARDEN) ROSES: Never treat a once-blooming rose like an everbloomer. Once-blooming roses and hardy old garden roses should be treated like other shrubs with summer-flowering shoots and pruned immediately after they produce a major flush of bloom. Generally, once-blooming roses are cut back only modestly to maintain a compact but open pattern of growth. On mature plants, you may find it helpful to remove older wood and canes that aren't blooming well with thinning cuts. Be sure to cut out enough canes to induce new ones. The increasingly popular rugosa roses (*Rosa rugosa*) respond especially well to a periodic removal of old canes. Old-fashioned roses often bloom only once during the summer, so deadheading faded blossoms may help extend the bloom.

THE RETURN OF ONCE-BLOOMING (SPECIES AND OLD GARDEN) ROSES: These roses are winning renewed popularity because of their har-

Before (after bloom): Remove old, disfigured, and diseased canes at the base with thinning cuts. Decorative rose hips (suitable for herb teas) can be retained or removed by deadheading.

After: Vigorous new growth emerges after pruning to replace the old canes that were removed. Annual pruning insures that the rose will be continually renewed.

ROSE ROSTER

Here is a selection of roses culled from the various categories presented in this chapter. For specific pruning advice, please consult the appropriate section. These cultivars have been chosen either for their ease of cultivation or remarkable beauty. When in doubt about pruning roses or which cultivars are applicable to your temperate zone, help is available. The American Rose Society has chapters located throughout the country, and they will often put you in contact with one of their consulting rosarians or a local rose enthusiast. As you would with other gardening questions, check with the Cooperative Extension Service, local nursery, or botanical gardens and arboretums in your area for additional information.

HYBRID TEA ROSES

'Blue Girl' (lavender)
'Brandy' (orange)
'Chicago Peace' (multicolor)
'Dainty Bess' (pink)
'Fragrant Cloud' (orange)
'Garden Party' (white)
'Lady Rose' (multicolor)
'Lady X' (lavender)
'Miss All-American Beauty'
   (pink)
'Mon Cheri' (multicolor)
'Mr. Lincoln' (red)
'Olympiad' (red)
'Paradise' (lavender)
'Peace' (yellow)
'Perfume Delight' (pink)
'Pristine' (white)
'Summer Sunshine' (yellow)
'Sutter's Gold' (yellow)
'White Masterpiece' (white)

ONCE-BLOOMING (SPECIES AND OLD GARDEN) ROSES

'Autumn Damask' (pink)
'Belle de Crécy' (pink)
'Camaieux' (crimson-pink)

'Cardinal de Richelieu' (purple)
'Celsiana' (pink)
'Charles de Mills'
   (purple, lavender)
'Comte de Chambord' (pink)
'd' Aguesseau' (crimson-rose)
'Duchesse de Brabant'
   (pearl-pink)
'Ispahan' (pink)
'Konigin von Danemark'
   (pink)
'La Ville de Bruxelles' (pink)
'Madame Hardy' (pink to white)
'Paul Neyron' (hot pink)
'Rosa Mundi'
   (striped pink/white)
Rosa soulieana (white)
'White Rose of York' (white)

FLORIBUNDA ROSES

'Apricot Nectar' (orange)
'Armada' (pink)
'Betty Prior' (pink)
'Escapade' (lavender)
'Europeana' (red)
'Golden Wings' (yellow)
'Iceberg' (white)
'Playboy' (orange-copper)

GRANDIFLORA ROSES

'Gold Medal' (yellow)
'Love' (red)
'Queen Elizabeth' (pink)
'Sundowner' (apricot)
'White Lightnin' ' (white)

ENGLISH ROSES (DAVID AUSTIN)

'Belle Story' (pink)
'Graham Thomas' (yellow)
'L.D. Braithwaite'
  (crimson-red)
'Othello' (purple)
'Winchester Cathedral'
  (white)

DWARF POLYANTHA ROSES

'Cecile Brunner' (pink)
'China Doll' (pink)
'The Fairy' (pink)
'Nathalie Nypels' (pink)
'Perle d' Or' (orange)
'White Pet' (white)

MINIATURE ROSES

'Baby Cecile Brunner'
  (pink)
'Beauty Secret' (red)
'Holy Toledo' (orange)
'Lavender Jewel' (lavender)
'Little Eskimo' (white)
'Opal Jewel' (pink)
'Peaches 'n Cream' (orange)
'Rise 'n Shine' (yellow)
'Toy Clown' (red)
'White Angel' (white)
'Yellow Doll' (yellow)

EXAMPLES OF RUGOSA ROSES

'Belle Poitevine' (lilac-pink)

'Blanc Double de Coubert'
  (white)
'Frau Dagmar Hartopp'
  (pale pink)
'Hansa' (purple-red)
Rosa rugosa 'Alba' (white)
Rosa rugosa 'Rubra'
  (blush wine)
'Scabrosa' (red-pink)

CLIMBING ROSES

'Altissimo' (red)
'Awakening' (silver-pink)
'Belle of Portugal'
  (salmon-pink)
'Cecile Brunner' climbing
  (pink)
'Constance Spry' (pink)
'Crimson Shower'
  (medium red)
'Dr. Van Fleet' (flesh-pink)
'Gardenia' (white)
'Gold Badge' climbing
  (yellow)
'Iceberg' climbing (white)
'John Davis' (rose)
'Kew Rambler' (pink)
'Lady Waterloo'
  (salmon-pink)
'Lavender Lassie'
  (lavender)
'Mermaid' (yellow)
'Mme. Alfred Carrière'
  (pearl-pink)
'New Dawn' (white)
'Paul Transon' (copper)
'Sander's White Rambler'
  (white)
'Souvenir de la Malmaison'
  climbing (pink)
'Veilchenblau' (mauve)
'Zephirine Drouhin' (rose)

diness and ability to adapt to various climates. In northern New England and the upper Midwest, for example, gardeners are once again coming to value the cold-tolerance of old-fashioned gallica, as well as many of the wild species roses. Both types are remarkably resistant to fungal diseases such as black spot, which plague the hybrid tea roses in areas with hot, humid summers.

MODERN SHRUB ROSES: You will find these roses listed in catalogs as "landscape roses," and it's an apt description since these roses are best used as landscaping shrubs to mass at the edge of a lawn or to arrange into a flowering hedge. Many varieties bloom repeatedly throughout the growing season, while others bloom only once. One group of old garden roses now gaining renewed popularity are the rugosa and hybrid rugosa. They share many characteristics with the modern shrub roses; they're exceptionally cold-hardy, disease resistant, and reliable rebloomers.

Prune all of these shrubs lightly to maintain a compact but open and healthy pattern of growth. Everblooming types should be pruned in early spring, while once-blooming types should be pruned after they flower. When planted as a flowering hedge, these shrub roses should be left to grow informally—trimming them into a formal hedge will eliminate most flowering.

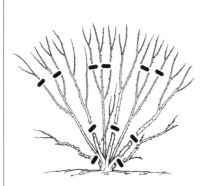

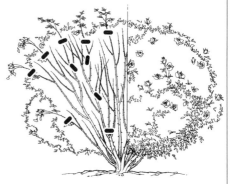

Before (dormant): Thin out spindly, damaged, diseased, or inward-growing canes. Cut older canes back to 6" for rejuvenation and thin the remainder back by ⅓ of their length.

After: Thin back overcrowded or excessively tall shoots as they can prevent steady growth and hinder air flow to the plant's interior. Remove spent flower trusses to encourage rebloom.

OTHER ROSES TO PRUNE AS SHRUBS: Though not usually classified as shrub roses, repeat bloomers such as floribunda, grandiflora, dwarf polyantha, David Austin, and miniature roses respond well to shrublike treatment. If they are pruned as shrub roses, they will make well-formed flowering shrubs ideal for use as accents in a flower border or to integrate with other shrubs.

PRUNING FLORIBUNDA AND GRANDIFLORA ROSES: Floribunda and grandiflora roses grow stronger, healthier, and hardier than hybrid tea roses. (Grandifloras tend to be more vigorous than floribundas.) Their flowers are smaller than hybrid teas and bloom continuously throughout the season. Follow the basic guidelines for everblooming roses, but be sure to remove all spent flower trusses as they appear if you want to sustain blooming. In the summer, cut old, fading flower trusses back to the first healthy bud facing away from the middle of the plant. In the fall, late winter, or early spring, remove one-third of the previous season's growth, cutting old canes back to about 6" above the ground. Shoots that are thinner than a pencil rarely produce quality flowers and should be cut back hard.

PRUNING DWARF POLYANTHA ROSES: Follow the general guidelines for floribundas, but dwarf polyanthas do not need a heavy pruning to encourage growth. Remove one-fourth to one-third of the previous season's growth but leave as many new canes as possible. Dwarf polyantha roses tend to make lots of twiggy growth, so remove old or dead twigs regularly.

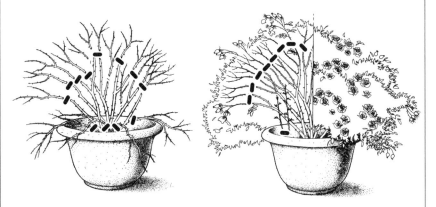

Before (dormant): Thin out crowded and unhealthy canes. Be sure to cut back older canes so the plant can renew itself with new growth.

After: Deadhead to remove spent flowers and head back canes that have flowered by ⅓. Remove any suckers that arise from the roots.

PRUNING MINIATURE ROSES: Treat miniature roses like you would a small floribunda rose. They're prone to many suckers because of their rootstock. If a miniature rose is grown from a cutting, the suckers will bloom true to the rest of the plant. If the rose was budded on a rootstock, however, remove the suckers as soon as they are spotted by digging down to the rootstock where the sucker originates and removing it.

CLIMBING ROSES: Climbing roses come in two types: climbers and ramblers. Climbers have pliable canes that can grow 50' or more into a tree and bloom in the spring *only* on two-year-old canes that grow from the base of the plant. Some climbers are actually hybrid tea "sports" that bloom intermittently throughout the spring and summer. Ramblers have big, stiff canes and don't twine easily around anything.

PRUNING CLIMBING ROSES: All climbing roses should be left unpruned, aside from the removal of damaged or dead tissue, for the first three years to build up vitality. The rose will begin to make large, vigorous canes and the blossoms appear on short laterals off the long canes. If the plant is left vertical, only a few blooms will develop near the tip of the cane. Bending the cane over an arch or horizontal over a fence will produce a tremendous amount of bloom. Sometimes the canes are staked to the ground to form a flowering ground cover of roses.

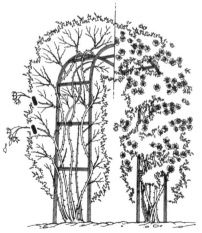

Before (dormant): On a mature climbing rose, thin back side branches to 2 or 3 buds, and remove old or unhealthy canes. Tie upright growth to the arch.

After: Once in full bloom, maintaining climbing roses is quite simple: vigilant deadheading, or removing spent flower trusses, insures a healthy plant.

PERENNIALS

Perennials are like expanding suburbs, enlarging their girth with more subdivisions each year. Many perennials die back to the ground by winter (or are cut to the ground by fastidious gardeners), but their talent for rejuvenation comes from their root structure, which multiplies to enlarge the clump. Despite their often aggressive habits, perennials remain a garden favorite because they are easy to divide and pass around to welcoming gardeners.

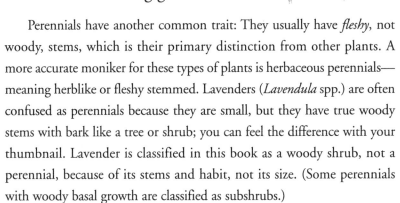

Perennials have another common trait: They usually have *fleshy*, not woody, stems, which is their primary distinction from other plants. A more accurate moniker for these types of plants is herbaceous perennials—meaning herblike or fleshy stemmed. Lavenders (*Lavendula* spp.) are often confused as perennials because they are small, but they have true woody stems with bark like a tree or shrub; you can feel the difference with your thumbnail. Lavender is classified in this book as a woody shrub, not a perennial, because of its stems and habit, not its size. (Some perennials with woody basal growth are classified as subshrubs.)

In most climates where lavender is grown, it's not cut flush to the ground like an herbaceous perennial. (In marginal climates, however, lavender is mulched for the winter and cut back severely in the spring.) A small variety of lavender called 'Munstead' or 'Munstead Dwarf' doesn't grow more than 12" tall.

In contrast to lavenders, tree dahlias (*Dahlia imperialis*) are tuberous-rooted perennials that grow very stiff stalks to 20' tall from a mass of underground tubers. The sturdy stems don't have true wood with rings like a tree, but tissue like a sunflower stalk that dies to the ground every fall. Thus, this towering beauty is classified as a perennial. Banana plants also fall into the category of perennials without true wood.

PINCHING: Part of the seasonal pruning for many herbaceous perennials involves pinching with fingernails (sometimes a clipper is used) or shearing. Pinching is the simple removal of many tip buds, which usually doubles the number of shoots by removing tip dominance. Pinch back growth to a well-placed dormant bud or set of opposing buds on each stem. Pinching is usually done in the spring prior to bloom in order to control the plant's shape and encourage bushiness. Stop pinching before flower buds begin to show. Among the plants often pinched to encourage bushiness are asters, bee balm, all forms of chrysanthemums, coleus, fuchsias, geraniums and pelargoniums, lantanas, poinsettias, red valerians, and salvias.

Pinch back the tops of annuals before you plant them to encourage bushier growth.

SHEARING: Shearing with hedge clippers for bushiness takes less time than pinching, but can leave foliage slightly ragged. Reserve shearing for herbaceous perennials with tight, small-leafed foliage or plants that quickly fill in their foliage. The foliage of the following plants is usually sheared: alpine chamomile, artemisias, candytuft, catmint, fleabane, lobelias, periwinkles, phlox, rue, santolinas, snow-in-summer, sweet woodruff, thymes, and yarrows. (If you're unsure, check with your local gardening club or neighbor-

Shear bushy flowers like Coreopsis verticillata *'Moonbeam' to remove the old flowers and encourage bushier growth.*

hood gardening mentor for more details. You may prune each plant differently compared to other gardeners—there is plenty of latitude for personal preference.)

DEADHEADING: Regardless of climate, many herbaceous perennials look much better with their spent blossoms removed by deadheading, although the practice tends to be a very personal decision. Fastidious gardeners carefully remove the dead blooms from nearly every plant. Gardeners who champion the natural or wild look, shy away from deadheading. Some natural gardeners make exceptions for especially shabby-looking dead blooms—such as yarrows (*Achillea* spp.) and Shasta daisy (*Chrysanthemum maximum*). A few plants, like bleeding hearts, will cooperate and naturally drop their flowers and stems in short order without any assistance from the gardener. Whether you opt for aesthetics or a more relaxed approach, deadheading prevents seed formation and prolongs bloom.

Deadhead most plants immediately after they finish blooming. Take care not to disturb the forming bud.

FALL CLEANUP . . . OR NOT: By the habit of the plant or by pruning at the hand of the gardener, perennials lose all their leaves, stalks, shoots, and stems in the fall. There are plenty of exceptions, though. In New England, for instance, the foliage of chrysanthemums is typically cut back to within 4" off the ground each fall; in mild coastal California areas, the same plant can be trimmed back to make it bushier, but the foliage is often left evergreen throughout the winter. Daylilies are also traditionally cut to the ground in the Midwest, but can be left as foliage throughout the winter in the milder Western gardens. (However, some daylilies are deciduous in all climates.)

Where the temperature falls below freezing in winter, most perennials are traditionally cut to the ground in the fall; however, leaving the dead flowers and foliage until spring is a more natural style. Uncut foliage catches snow to make a mulch, another type of landscape "structure" each winter. The spent foliage also provides cover for wildlife, and the old flowers offer seeds to winter-foraging birds and animals. Where winters are particularly hard on certain plants, some gardeners believe that leaving the spent foliage and flower heads lend a measure of winter protection to the plant. In most cases, gardeners tidy up the garden in spring and remove spent foliage.

In warm-winter areas, many plants are traditionally left as winter foliage accents and are sheared back only if the plant is getting too leggy to display the bloom properly; this pruning is usually done after blooming or in the early spring.

Common yarrow, Milfoil

BOTANICAL NAME: *Achillea millefolium*

PLANT TYPE: Perennial

SIZE: Grows to 2½' tall. Species vary from 2"–6" (*A. tomentosa*) to 3' (*A. filipendulina*).

GROWING HABITS: Fast-growing with rain or irrigation. Slower-growing under drought conditions, but will tolerate low water. Spreads sideways by underground rhizomes.

TIME TO PRUNE: Shear back hard in the summer after bloom. On ornamental varieties, cut back flowering stems after bloom, which may cause reblooming.

NEW SHOOTS AFTER CUTTING BARE STEMS? Does not apply.

SPECIAL PRUNING POINTERS: *A. millefolium* can be used somewhat like an alternative lawn, but tolerates very little foot traffic.

STEP BY STEP: *1.* In all climates, prune, shear, or mow quite low after bloom. *2.* Divide in fall or early spring as needed, when crowns are crowded.

Fennel

BOTANICAL NAME: *Foeniculum vulgare*

PLANT TYPE: Perennial

SIZE: Grows 3'–5' tall, up to 4' wide.

GROWING HABITS: Fast-growing in spring from root. Evergreen foliage in mild-winter areas. Makes a fountain of light green to chartreuse foliage with bright yellow umbel flowers in mid-summer. The ornamental variety, *F. vulgare dulce* var. *rubrum* (called bronze fennel), has an unusual dark purplish black foliage with metallic overtones. (Bronze fennel is a short-lived perennial in subzero-winter areas where it is often treated as an annual.)

Fennel *(continued)*

TIME TO PRUNE: Summer pruning of flower heads. Fall removal of foliage.

NEW SHOOTS AFTER CUTTING BARE STEMS? Does not apply.

SPECIAL PRUNING POINTERS: This plant can get weedy if seeds are left to mature. Cut flower heads off after most of their blossoms have finished. Seeds make good bird food.

STEP BY STEP: *1.* In any climate, cut back all foliage to the ground in fall. (In mild-winter areas, trim out dead flower and leaf stalks in fall and leave any good-looking foliage for winter color.) *2.* If foliage is left over the winter, cut to the ground in early spring. *3.* Before the umbel flower heads finish blooming, cut flower stalks back to their base to prevent ripe seed from scattering.

Before: As fennel flowers fade, the entire flowering stalk can be cut down to healthy lower foliage. If seeds are allowed to mature, they may self sow and become weedy.

After: Fennel foliage looks healthy and vigorous without the fading flower stalk and the energy drain of seed production.

VINES

Most gardens are greatly enhanced by the judicious use of deciduous or evergreen vines. They are very effective at covering large walls or cloak- 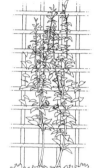 ing ugly architecture. They spill foliage and blossom when growing up a tree, offer wonderful fragrances, give height to the garden, dress up a pergola, or even grow as a ground cover.

Generally, vines are defined by how they climb or attach themselves to a support structure. There are four major types of vines: rambling, twining, clinging, and those that climb with tendrils.

The wildest forms, *rambling* vines, act almost like large, leggy, floppy shrubs if left untended. Some of these vines lean onto large plants, while others support themselves by thorns. Rambling vines, as a rule, must be tied to a support to gain any real height, like some climbing roses (*Rosa* spp.), which are deciduous rambling vines.

Less wild, but still rambunctious, are the groping vines that sprawl over the garden. Called *twining* vines for obvious reasons, they climb by roughly wrapping their long, young shoots around arbors and trellises or through neighboring plants.

The ivy-covered buildings of Harvard University display *clinging* vines. These persistent growers use little sucker pads (in the case of evergreen ivies) or aerial roots to grab surfaces.

Tendril vines have leafless, curling shoots that wrap around objects to climb. Tendril vines can climb rapidly without any help from the gardener. It's more likely that you'll need to restrain the extent of their growth rather than encourage it.

DECIDUOUS VINES

Deciduous vines offer the added pleasure of some fruiting varieties, but will ultimately become bare, dying back to the ground or shedding their foliage, as winter approaches in cold climates. Deciduous vines can be either herbaceous (soft-stemmed) or woody.

Popular deciduous twining vines include Kolomikta (*Actinidia kolomikta*), the ornamental relative of the fruiting kiwi, five-leaved akebia (*Akebia quinata*), silver lace vine (*Polygonum aubertii*), and the ever-popular wisteria (*Wisteria* spp.). Some twining varieties, like the silver lace vine, do not show many of the growth and flowering characteristics of woody trees and shrubs common to twining vines, and will flower readily on all shoots and in all positions. Other types, most notably wisteria, form spurs on second-year growth much like a flowering or fruiting tree, although the position of the shoots is not important.

Some deciduous vines, especially tendril-climbing varieties like gourds (*Cucurbita* spp.), use more than one method to climb. Other popular vines in this category include coral vine (*Antigonon leptopus*) and ornamental and edible grapes (*Vitis* spp.).

The particular habit of clinging vines makes them ideal for covering large surfaces. Common trumpet vines (*Campsis* spp.) and climbing hydrangeas (*Hydrangea anomala*) are popular representatives of deciduous vines.

PRUNING BY TYPE: As a general rule, all spring-blooming vines are pruned immediately after blooming, while summer- and fall-blooming vines are pruned the following spring, just before bud break. However, each of the four vining categories varies with regard to pruning.

Wild, unruly vines, or ramblers, can be left to grow unrestrained, but only if you have a huge garden that can accommodate the space they'll usurp. Tall, vertical growth can be slowed down by bending or tying it down to encourage more branching—but again, space is a prerequisite, so prune and tie without restraint. You may have to prune an abandoned plant back considerably in order to tie it to a support. Be sure to use sturdy garden tape to secure rambling vines to a trellis, arbor, or pergola. Once the vine is attached, use thinning cuts to its branch collar to remove all unwanted growth. After the volume of growth has been reduced, use heading cuts on the untied shoots to encourage side shoots or bloom. In warm-winter areas, prune summer- and fall-flowering vines back in the fall or winter, but prune them in spring where winters are harsh.

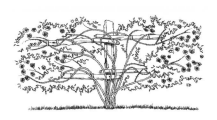

Rambling roses have long, trailing branches that can be tied onto trellises or fences.

Twining vines, like kiwi, wrap around supporting stakes, fences, and branches.

Tendril-climbing vines, such as grapes, use modified stems that hold onto supporting trellises or trees.

Clinging vines, like Virginia creeper, have suction-cuplike holdfasts that stick to walls, trunks, and other upright objects.

Like most plants, vines can make sucker growth at the base of the plant. If the growth comes from below the bud on a grafted rootstock, it will not have the same characteristics as the top of the plant and should be removed as soon as it is noticed. If the vine was grown from a cutting, the suckers will be identical to the rest of the plant and can be used to rejuvenate the overall plant.

Follow the same general guidelines when pruning twining vines that are recommended for vines with a wild habit. You won't have to pay as much attention to tying, except for wayward shoots that can't find a support on their own. When growing a vine for its foliage, you can shear it back often during the summer to just about any depth or shape (be forewarned though, this can be a time-consuming task depending on the particular habit of the vine). The silver lace vine and the hop vine (*Humulus lupulus*), for example, can even be cut to the ground each winter without harm to the plant, but summer bloom is delayed to late summer.

Deciduous clematis vines come with many different growth and flowering patterns and use twisting leaf stems, called petioles, to climb various surfaces with modest success. Some, such as *Clematis orientalis, C. tangutica, C. texensis,* and *C. viticella,* bear flowers only on new growth in late summer and require severe pruning to the lowest pair of healthy buds. Some spring pruning may be needed to stimulate new shoots that will flower in the second year.

Tendril vines need even less attention than twining varieties. They are more likely to grow vertically without care—providing there's some support or another plant to climb. Prune them in summer for removal of unwanted growth and in fall or spring to provoke shoots. Grapes will fruit on spurs located on two-year-old growth and are pruned much like apple and pear trees.

Clinging vines grow rapidly to cover vertical walls. A vine like Virginia creeper (*Parthenocissus quiquefolia*) is revered for its foliage, especially in the fall. And light shearing during the summer will not interfere with the fall display. Ivies are grown for their foliage and can be pruned in spring to force new shoots or in summer to control wayward shoots; both methods encourage thicker, more luxurious growth. Don't prune too late in summer where winters are harsh, as any new growth will not have time to harden for the winter months. Pruning in late summer can also invite disease in some climates.

Japanese wisteria, Chinese wisteria, Silky wisteria

BOTANICAL NAMES: *Wisteria floribunda, W. sinensis, W. venusta*

PLANT TYPE: Deciduous Vine

SIZE: Old vines left to grow uninhibited can climb more than 100' up a tree. Can be trained to a trellis of any size or as a standard "tree."

GROWING HABITS: Rampant vine with spur systems for flowering. Blooms profusely if unpruned, but needs plenty of space for large mature size.

TIME TO PRUNE: Winter pruning is typical and is the best time to discern flowering growth from the vining vegetative growth. Summer pruning of the long twining growth will help control the plant's size.

NEW SHOOTS AFTER CUTTING BARE STEMS? Will sprout new shoots from buds on old, bare growth. Abandoned plants can be restored by massive pruning in the winter to encourage vigor and subsequent summer pruning to tame any overly vigorous growth.

Japanese wisteria, Chinese wisteria, Silky wisteria *(continued)*

SPECIAL PRUNING POINTERS: The flowering spurs are quite noticeable with their large, fat buds on short, stubby growth. You can train this vine to fit just about any shaped trellis, arbor, or pergola if you leave behind enough laterals that can be pruned into flowering spurs in the summer. Begin pruning for flowering spurs by trimming back long laterals to about 6" around midsummer. Then cut to two or three buds in late fall or early winter. If you have more time, cut back all unwanted vegetative lateral growth to 6" or three leaves every two or three weeks in the summer to force more lateral growth, which should also be pruned back to 6". In winter, thin out any laterals or any other unwanted growth you missed in the summer.

Wisteria vines can also be trellised like fruiting grape vines or espalier fruit trees. For the first tier on a wire trellis, hold the desired lateral growth to a 45° angle during the first summer. This will encourage the formation of flower buds and spurs. These can be tied horizontally the following winter for a formal espalier pattern. Maintain a central leader from which two shoots are chosen as the next tier. Each tier is trained the same way as the first.

STEP BY STEP: *1.* Plant a grafted variety of wisteria for reliable blossom color. (Grafted plants also typically flower at a younger age.) *2.* No need to prune if the vine is to be trained to an arbor, high trellis, or pergola. Just plant and prune off all lower foliage in late summer. Winter is a good time to establish a skeleton of primary branches, or to shape the plant into a space as it matures. *3.* Use summer pruning to reduce the growth of vigorous twining shoots to 6" stubs. The more this is

done, the greater the flower-bud formation. In late summer, cut all stubbed-back laterals to two or three buds for the final push for flower growth.

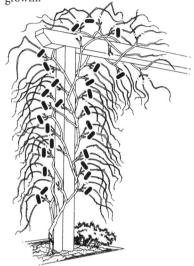

Before (dormant): Cut back unwanted growth to the knobby flower buds.

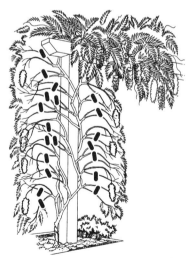

After (summer pruning): Using heading cuts, remove the nonflowering side branches back to 6" stubs. Later in the season, cut branches back farther to 2 or 3 buds.

Common trumpet vine, Trumpet creeper

BOTANICAL NAME: *Campsis radicans*

PLANT TYPE: Deciduous Vine

SIZE: Grows to 40'; give plenty of room.

GROWING HABITS: Clinging vine that flowers in mid to late summer on current season's growth (summer-flowering shoots). Flowers best in full sun.

TIME TO PRUNE: In the fall after bloom or early spring.

NEW SHOOTS AFTER CUTTING BARE STEMS? Will sprout new shoots from trace buds on old growth, but best to cut back to an existing node or shoot.

SPECIAL PRUNING POINTERS: In cold-winter areas, this vine will be killed to the ground, so cut it to 6"-stubs in the fall after bloom is over and mulch. In mild-winter areas, the vines will over-winter and can be pruned hard or never pruned. Because the blooms are born on summer-flowering shoots, you'll get flowering regardless of how heavily or softly you prune. Old unattended vines can get so bulky they will pull away from the wall or trellis (they have been known to collapse a barn).

STEP BY STEP: Three options: *1.* Never prune. *2.* Prune as little or as much as you like. *3.* Cut to the ground each fall.

EVERGREEN VINES

Evergreen vines should be treated similarly to deciduous vines; prune spring-flowering evergreen vines immediately after blooming. The new growth that forms will be the tip-blooming growth of the following spring. Late summer- and fall-blooming vines can be pruned the following spring because they bloom on new terminal growth (shoots of the current season). Leave spent flowers or foliage on the plants to help protect against winter's bitter cold. In warm-winter climates, fall pruning or shearing of late-blooming vines is possible, but you risk damage to new growth from rare or occasional frosts.

Broadly speaking, many of the spring- and summer-blooming evergreen vines can be sheared or pruned rather heavily to restrain their growth. Quite a few can be cut back into bare growth and still make plenty of new shoots. Check with a nurseryperson about your specific vine.

Conversely, most of these vines can also be left to grow completely untended with profuse, reliable bloom at their outer edge. Don't forget to give abandoned vines considerable space horizontally or vertically, depending upon their growth habit.

In dry areas of the West, allowing vines to conquer much of the house or garage is a considerable fire hazard. Even though Japanese honeysuckle is

EVERGREEN VINES

RAMBLING EVERGREEN VINES

Bougainvilleas (*Bougainvillea* spp.)

Cup-of-gold vine
(*Solandra maxima*)

Fatshedera (*Fatshedera lizei*)

Jasmine, Angelwing
(*Jasminum nitidum*)

Plumbago, Cape
(*Plumbago auriculata*)

Raspberries and **Blackberries**
(*Rubus* spp.) (in warm-winter
areas)

Roses, climbing (*Rosa* spp.)

Wax flower (*Hoya carnosa*)

TWINING EVERGREEN VINES

Chilean bellflower (*Lapageria rosea*)

Glorybower, Bleeding heart
(*Clerodendrum thomsoniae*)

Hardenbergias (*Hardenbergia* spp.)

Herald's trumpet, Easter lily vine
(*Beaumontia grandiflora*)

Jasmine, Common white
(*Jasminum officinale*)

Jasmine, Pink
(*J. polyanthum*)

Potato vine (*Solanum jasminoides*)

Silver lace vine (*Polygonum aubertii*)
(Evergreen in warm-winter
climates.)

Star jasmine
(*Trachelospermum jasminoides*)

Thunbergia vines
(*Thunbergia* spp.)

CLINGING EVERGREEN VINES

Fig, Creeping (*Ficus pumila*)

Ivies: Algerian (*Hedera canariensis*)
Baltic (*H. helix 'Baltica'*)
English (*H. helix*)
Persian (*H. colchica*)

Wintercreeper (*Euonymus fortunei*)

EVERGREEN VINES WITH TENDRILS

Clematis, Evergreen
(*Clematis armandii*)

Flame vine
(*Pyrostegia venusta*)

Ivies: Boston
(*Parthenocissus tricuspidata*)
Grape (*Cissus rhombifolia*)
Oak leaf (*Rhoicissus capensis*)

Passion vines, Hybrid
passionflowers (*Passiflora* spp.)

Queen's wreath, Coral vine
(*Antigonon leptopus*)

Trumpet vine, Blood-red
(*Distictis buccinatoria*)

Trumpet vine, Yellow
(*Anemopaegma chamberlaynii*)

an evergreen in mild-winter climates, for example, a tremendous amount of
dead vines builds up under the thin layer of evergreen foliage. One drifting
ember from a nearby fire will set the accumulated dry twigs on fire like they
were gasoline. In fire-prone areas, plant only vines that require or tolerate
a severe yearly pruning to eliminate all spent growth on the house's walls.

Evergreen clematis

BOTANICAL NAME: *Clematis armandii*

PLANT TYPE: Evergreen Vine

SIZE: Grows to 20'.

GROWING HABITS: Once established, a fast-growing vine that climbs by tendrils. Bears white, fragrant blossoms on second-year-flowering shoots early in the spring. Leaves are dark green and glossy and are composed of three leaflets on a long stem. The stems of each leaf cluster spring from opposite sides of the vine.

TIME TO PRUNE: Trim hard after bloom to control the buildup of old shoots. Because it's a second-year-flowering vine, it can be sheared back considerably as long as you are careful to leave enough two-year-old shoots for flower the following year. Can be pinched in the summer to help control size.

NEW SHOOTS AFTER CUTTING BARE STEMS? Cut back only to a node where two leaf stems or shoots join the vine or to the base of major vining lateral.

SPECIAL PRUNING POINTERS: Treat like any other tendril vine. Give it something to grasp for vertical growth. Even though it will bloom quite well if left alone, don't allow to go uncut. Abandoned vines have rangy foliage on top and a pile of dead shoots beneath. With pruning, be firm, but not brutal.

STEP BY STEP: *1.* Tie young vines to a supporting trellis. Tie tips you want to grow higher above all other vines. This promotes tip-bud dominance for faster vertical growth. *2.* After pruning for the basic shape once the bloom is over, you can encourage more vertical growth by cutting back from the main vine(s) to one bud of the previous season's growth. *3.* To control height, cut out the vertical shoots at a stem or shoot node.

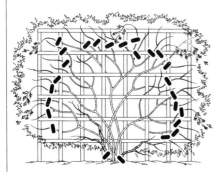

Before: In late spring, as flowers are fading, shear to limit size and thin back old or damaged wood.

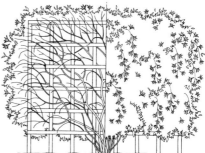

After: Flowers will bloom the following spring primarily on last year's new growth, but also on older side shoots.

Japanese honeysuckle (evergreen in mild-winter areas)

BOTANICAL NAME: *Lonicera japonica*

PLANT TYPE: Evergreen Vine

SIZE: Climbs to 15' or more and can spread up to 150 square feet.

GROWING HABITS: A vigorous, twining evergreen vine that bears fragrant blossoms in late spring or early summer on the current season's growth (terminal-flowering shoots). Aggressive and invasive. Has escaped from cultivation and is a noxious alien weed in many areas—smothers and crowds out native species.

TIME TO PRUNE: Prune heavily after bloom to contain. Summer pruning can be used to remove unwanted long twining shoots.

NEW SHOOTS AFTER CUTTING BARE STEMS? Cut back only to a node where leaves are joined to the vine or to the base of a major vining lateral.

SPECIAL PRUNING POINTERS: Will thrive without pruning, but outer foliage can be rangy. Tremendous amounts of dead vines and shoots build up beneath the green foliage—a real fire hazard in the arid West.

STEP BY STEP: (With an abandoned vine needing restoration, start at the top or outer edges and roughly shear back the bulk of the unwanted foliage.) *1.* Use hand clippers or loppers to remove to the base any long, unwanted old vines, leaving the newer, healthier vines. *2.* Use hand clippers to custom-trim all remaining shoots to a pair of leaves or another shoot. Tie to the trellis, pergola, or arbor.

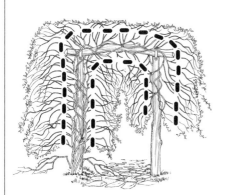

Before (dormant): An overgrown, abandoned honeysuckle vine can be invigorated by shearing off excessive growth, thinning out old, dead, and overcrowded stems, and trimming remaining shoots back to a pair of leaves or a side shoot.

After: The resulting vine has fewer main vine stems and healthy new growth. It will need continued pruning for maintenance.

HEDGES

While many people believe that hedges have drifted into cliché, they serve all kinds of marvelous functions. If they are well planned and trained with a creative eye toward style, they are one of the most effective landscape devices in the gardener's repertoire.

The common hedge—whether deciduous or evergreen—is anything but common. Its versatility and practicality are timeless. If used correctly, hedges are the "bones" of any garden: they screen off unwanted views; provide privacy from neighbors; they have a grand tradition as the neutral backdrop for flower borders and other landscape features; they act as a living barrier—especially the really prickly plants—to some roaming animals and people; they shape and define movement throughout the garden as well as frame the views within and out of a garden; and they can shelter part of your yard from harsh winds or protect it from snow by what is often called a shelterbelt or snowcatch. The right plants can funnel cooling winds into sunny, warm places in the yard or define a part of it like an outdoor room. Lastly, a tall and wide hedge may reduce the *psychological* impact of noise (only a really thick broadleaf hedgerow blocks *some* sound).

The hedge as cliché occurs when it is planted arbitrarily, without a sense of design or any botanical style. And even a well-designed hedge is a waste of space if it's not pruned properly. Timely pruning will maintain the texture, shape, and function for which the hedge was intended. And while hedges and shrubs are examined separately in this book, many shrubs can be trained as hedges quite easily.

DECIDUOUS HEDGES

Pruning deciduous hedges is rather straightforward, but shearing a hedge, with or without a powered hedge clipper, takes elbow grease, patience, and sweat. The more geometrically precise you want the hedge, the greater the pruning effort in both frequency and attention to detail.

Many common deciduous hedges, such as barberry, Russian olive, and some viburnums, are valued for just their foliage. Since bloom is irrelevant with these hedges, the season of pruning is not important. With other deciduous hedges, such as lilac and pomegranate, gardeners want to have both clipped foliage and a colorful flower display. Pruning these hedges requires more consideration about timing. Nonetheless, most hedges (especially those for privacy) are meant to have foliage from the ground up.

Hedges for foliage, not flower, need yearly or frequent pruning to temporarily remove the influence of the tip bud and stimulate side shoots that make the foliage appear thicker and denser.

DECIDUOUS HEDGES GROWN FOR THEIR FOLIAGE

Barberries (*Berberis* spp.)

Buckthorn, Alder
  (*Rhamnus frangula* 'Columnaris')

Cranberry bush, European
  (*Viburnum opulus* 'Nanum')
  (also for flower)

Honeysuckle (*Lonicera korolkowii*)

Honeysuckle, Fragrant or **Winter**
  (*L. fragrantissima*)

Honeysuckle, Tatarian (*L. tatarica*)

Hornbeam, European
  (*Carpinus betulus*)

Osage orange (*Maclura pomifera*)

Osier, Purple; Alaska blue willow
  (*Salix purpurea* 'Gracilis')

Privet, Common
  (*Ligustrum vulgare*)

Siberian pea shrub
  (*Caragana arborescens*)
  (also for flower)

PRUNING DECIDUOUS HEDGES: In cold climates, prune the day all dormant plants are planted to induce new growth close to the ground. In warm-winter areas, however, plants in full leaf can be planted in the fall. You can clip back small plants to 6" above the soil to encourage foliage from the ground up. Often, it's wise to leave the tip bud on the central leader intact, thereby speeding up vertical growth until the hedge reaches the desired height. Once this happens, clip back the tip bud to control the height of the hedge.

Regardless of climate, clip or shear the following summer when growth gets long. The more often you clip, the tighter and denser the foliage will appear. It's often recommended to cut back about one-third of the new growth, but this depends on how many side shoots you want to produce. Harder pruning—more than one-third of the new growth—will make a denser hedge. Always consider how fast a plant is growing and how much time you have to devote to pruning when making decisions about hedges.

In cold-winter areas, do not trim too late in summer and risk delaying the normal dormancy period of the plant. In fact, leaving the hedge a little long before winter may add a slight measure of winter protection and you can begin shearing when all danger of frost has passed in the spring. In warm-winter climates, you can prune up to and even past the typical time for the last summer pruning.

Repeated yearly shearing can lead to a stiff look and a large zone of dead shoots on the interior covered by a thin exterior of foliage. To avoid this effect, follow shear-

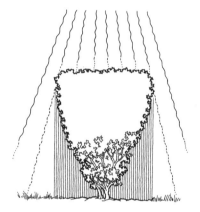

The top of an improperly pruned hedge shades the lower portion and thus stunts the growth of foliage near the ground.

ing with selective hand pruning of ragged edges—to open up the hedge to sunlight and a less rigid exterior—every two or three years.

Make sure you plan the hedge to be no wider than twice your comfortable reach—without excessive bending or stretching—from the ladder. The wise gardener keeps a hedge's width equal to one convenient arm's reach to avoid moving the ladder up and down both sides of the hedge, which is both time-consuming and can result in an uneven hedge. Also, shaping the top of the hedge to be narrower than the bottom will allow better penetration of sunlight and keep the lower portion of the hedge healthy.

As the hedge begins to mature, gardeners wishing to have a very geometric hedge may want to set up twine or boards for pruning to define the shape of the hedge, but be attentive because twine is easily clipped along with the foliage. Using guides will allow for a very level top and perfectly angular sides.

When using an electric hedge clipper, always drag the power cord over the same shoulder or around the side of the waist that you're holding the clipper. Grasp a small loop of cord in the hand that carries the weight of the clippers. This practice will help you to be constantly aware of the location of the power cord so you don't cut it.

Common lilac

BOTANICAL NAME: *Syringa vulgaris*

PLANT TYPE: Deciduous Hedge

SIZE: Can reach 20' if unpruned. Pruning can keep it down to 3'–5'.

GROWING HABITS: Typical spring-flowering shrub with a wondrous scent in full bloom. Flowers on tips of second-year shoots. Flower buds form in pairs where the leaves join the shoots. Lilac can be planted 2½'–3' apart for a solid hedge.

TIME TO PRUNE: Spring pruning will destroy the bloom. Prune after blossoms have faded through midsummer.

NEW SHOOTS AFTER CUTTING BARE STEMS? Cut into bare branches (stems) to generate new growth. This is important when trying to restore portions of a hedge or plant.

SPECIAL PRUNING POINTERS: After bloom, cut spent flower clusters to just above where the new buds are forming. Don't allow the flowers to mature their seed. You must control the tips of vigorous shoots with summer pruning; use thinning cuts to remove to their origin if the hedge has plenty of foliage. If the hedge's foliage is sparse, the vigorous shoots can be clipped

Before: As lilac flowers fade, remove them before the seeds mature. Shape the hedge as needed.

After: During the summer, remove suckers and dead or diseased wood, and thin back crowded or lanky stems.

Common lilac *(continued)*

back to just below the top of the hedge and encouraged to make laterals. Repeated heading of once wayward vertical shoots can fill in holes in the hedge. Any shoots from the rootstock should be removed in mid to late summer as some lilacs are grafted and the rootstock won't have the same beauty as the lilac cultivar you bought; in fact, it may be another plant altogether, like privet. However, more and more lilacs are grown on their own roots.

STEP BY STEP: *1.* Shape the hedge after bloom. Shear with hedge clippers if the hedge is big or long. Some forming flower buds may be lost but it'll take much less time. *2.* Remove shoots that grow well above the top of the hedge with selective summer pruning.

Red-leaf Japanese barberry

BOTANICAL NAME: *Berberis thunbergii* 'Atropurpurea'

PLANT TYPE: Deciduous Hedge

SIZE: As a shrub, grows 4'–6' tall and wide. Can be kept below 4' as a hedge.

GROWING HABITS: This reddish purple or bronze leaf (if grown in full sun) form is grown for its unique and attractive foliage, so there's no conflict with pruning to maintain blossoms. Will make some small yellow flowers followed by bright red berries even when sheared into a hedge. Slow-growing.

TIME TO PRUNE: Since flower is not the goal, shear anytime. Clip in the spring to remove the tip buds on shoots to form more side shoots for a fuller hedge. Use hand pruners to summer prune wildly growing shoots. Use thinning cuts to control vigorous wayward shoots. By mid to late summer, do the last shearing to shape the hedge for the winter season, but since this plant is deciduous, the final pruning isn't critical.

NEW SHOOTS AFTER CUTTING BARE STEMS? Cutting to older bare shoots is fine to sprout new growth.

SPECIAL PRUNING POINTERS: Spiny growth makes barberry a good barrier plant, but tough on the unprepared pruner. Wear a long-sleeved shirt and thorn-resistant gloves.

Before: In spring, head back skimpy branches to encourage gap-filling growth. You also can shear to shape, wearing gloves as protection from spines.

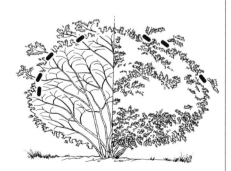

After: In summer, thin out fast-growing wayward shoots.

Red-leaf Japanese barberry *(continued)*

STEP BY STEP: *1.* Plant 15"–24" apart for a hedge. Prune close to ground after planting to encourage multiple shoots from the ground up. *2.* Head back rigorously or as needed in the spring or early summer to thicken the foliage. *3.* Every year or two, renew bare sections of the hedge by cutting poor-growing, three- to four-year-old shoots to the ground in early spring. This will force new shoots that are more colorful than older branches. Head new shoots as needed to fill in any bare spots.

EVERGREEN HEDGES

Evergreen hedges—usually grown for their shady canopies—make up for what deciduous hedges lack in winter. They're great year-round for screening out nosy neighbors, the auto-wreck yard next door, or the air-conditioner unit behind the garage.

Gardeners in warm-winter climates have many choices of evergreen hedges, including many "edible hedges" such as all varieties of citrus (*Citrus* spp.), loquat (*Eriobotrya japonica*), natal plum (*Carissa grandiflora*), pineapple guava (*Feijoa sellowiana*), and strawberry guava (*Psidium cattleianum*). These terminal-bearing plants make great informal or casual edible hedges because the seasonal shearing doesn't eliminate all the branch tips, allowing new growth to bear fruit in late summer through fall. Casually kept hedges of terminal-bearing plants will have more fruit than severely pruned formal hedges. There are no acceptable edible evergreen hedges for colder climates, and the choice of inedible hedges is restricted as well.

EVERGREEN HEDGES FOR COLD-WINTER CLIMATES

Douglas fir
   (*Pseudotsuga menziesii*)
Hemlock, Canadian
   (*Tsuga canadensis*)
Hollies (*Ilex* spp.)
Junipers (*Juniperus* spp.)
Pine, White
   (*Pinus strobus*)
Rhododendrons
   (*Rhododendron* spp.)
Spruce, Norway
   (*Picea abies*)
Spruce, White
   (*P. glauca*)
Yew, Japanese
   (*Taxus cuspidata*)

PRUNING EVERGREEN HEDGES: Prune evergreen hedges as you would deciduous hedges, but avoid pruning too late in the summer as new growth is more susceptible to early freezes. Pruning evergreen hedges to a formal shape, however, requires more attention to detail than deciduous hedges. The evergreen foliage shows pruning defects more easily and mistakes last all winter long. For precision, a scaffold or a guide made of string, wood, or metal is required.

EVERGREEN HEDGES GROWN FOR THEIR FOLIAGE

Boxwoods, Common (some)
  (*Buxus* spp.)
Carob or **St. John's bread**
  (*Ceratonia siliqua*)
Cedars, Arborvitaes (*Thuja* spp.)
Cherry, Hollyleaf (*Prunus ilicifolia*)
Cotoneasters (some) (*Cotoneaster*)
Cypresses (*Cupressus* spp.)
Euonymus, Evergreen
  (*Euonymus japonica*)
Hawthorn, India
  (*Rhaphiolepis indica*)

Hemlocks (*Tsuga* spp.)
Junipers (*Juniperus* spp.)
  (shrub and column types)
Laurel, Carolina
  (*Prunus caroliniana*)
Laurel, English
  (*P. laurocerasus*)
Photinias (*Photinia* spp.)
Privets (*Ligustrum* spp.)
Viburnums
  (*Viburnum* spp.) (some)
Yews (*Taxus* spp.)

The old garden term for the device used to measure and set the angle of a hedge to be sheared is a "batter." The plumb bob is used to keep the vertical element perpendicular to the ground and the other two boards are slid against each other and bolted together to the proper angle. For small hedges (under 4' tall), a permanently shaped template can be constructed to guide the pruner to all the correct angles.

Japanese boxwood

BOTANICAL NAME: *Buxus microphylla* var. *japonica*

PLANT TYPE: Evergreen Hedge

SIZE: Grows up to 8' tall and wide without pruning. Can be kept as low as 6". More often clipped to 1'–4' wide.

GROWING HABITS: Reliable, time-proven hedge. Slow to moderate growth, but faster than other species of *Buxus*. Bright, vivid green, compact leaves make this foliage an all-American favorite for hedges. Branches form

Japanese boxwood *(continued)*

easily without shearing and will do so in abundance with clipping. Flowers are unimpressive; prune for foliage form.

TIME TO PRUNE: Prune after last frost and anytime during the summer when growth is too rangy to suit your style. In cold climates, be sure to stop pruning well before the first hard freezes to avoid succulent, vulnerable growth. (If the tender shoots from late pruning haven't hardened before the first frost, prune the tips off the hedge.)

NEW SHOOTS AFTER CUTTING BARE STEMS? Cut to any old growth and it will sprout readily.

SPECIAL PRUNING POINTERS: This plant's special virtue is its adaptability to just about any form or size under 6'. Pick a shape and prune.

STEP BY STEP: *1.* At minimum, shear the sides of the hedge. (Keep the leader uncut if you want the hedge to grow tall quickly.)

All shearing removes the tip-bud dominance, which will stimulate more laterals and denser foliage. *2.* Once you have a shape in mind (remember, a healthy hedge is wider at the bottom than the top), prune the hedge when it gets too overgrown for your liking. Use a wooden template or a set of strings or boards to mark the edges of the hedge to guide your shears. In areas with winter snow, it may accumulate deep enough to break shoots and branches if the hedge is too dense. A more open canopy will allow snow to filter through to the ground and reduce breakage. *3.* If disease causes a hole in the hedge, cut back all dead or diseased growth to clean, green shoots or branches. Plant a replacement in the hole and encourage faster growth with extra water and fertilizer.

Use a wooden frame to neatly shear a formal hedge of Japanese boxwood.

Canadian or Eastern hemlock

BOTANICAL NAME: *Tsuga canadensis*

PLANT TYPE: Evergreen Hedge

SIZE: Without pruning, grows to 40'–70' tall and to 35' wide. Can be clipped to any height between 4'–20'.

GROWING HABITS: Slow-growing conifer. Naturally forms a central leader with a broad conical shape and slightly drooping branches on unpruned trees. Branches easily when the tip buds are clipped off. Finely textured, dark green foliage (yellowish tint to spring growth) makes an excellent mid-sized hedge. One of the best cold-tolerant hedges, it tolerates temperatures down to approximately −25°F.

TIME TO PRUNE: Anytime after spring growth has begun. Shear often enough to make sure you are cutting into the new growth. A later summer pruning

For big jobs, like a Canadian hemlock hedge, use electric hedge shears (with the cord safely looped over your shoulder) and a sturdy ladder.

will help maintain a dense, firm-textured surface to the hedge for winter's wind, snow, or ice. Mature hemlock hedges may only need a clipping in late summer.

NEW SHOOTS AFTER CUTTING BARE STEMS? Don't let this hedge go so long that you are forced to cut into bare growth that will not fill in.

SPECIAL PRUNING POINTERS: Fills in so densely that this is a good candidate for an architecturally shaped hedge. Use templates, twine, or boards for shearing guides.

STEP BY STEP: *1.* Plant in either spring or fall from containers. For a tight hedge, plant 1½'–5' apart. Do not clip the leader. Lightly cut back any scraggly growth. Tie loosely to a stake if the trunk is too spindly, but allow it to flex with the wind to help build strength. *2.* From the second year until the central leader gets to the desired height, trim all lateral growth to match whatever shape you choose. Leave the central leader untouched. *3.* Once the leader reaches the preferred height of the hedge, cut the central leader out with summer pruning.

SHRUBS

Shrubs, along with trees, are the backbone of the garden border and home landscape. As such, they have a special value and are often the first plants set in the ground when constructing a new garden. They give form to the winter garden and provide welcome blooms in spring and summer. Shrubs should be treated the same as most plants at first; cut off all dead or damaged shoots, branches, or limbs as soon as you see them. Be sure to always cut them back to the healthy branch collar of a side shoot or limb and leave the branch collar intact. Be on the lookout for disease (fire blight, olive knot, or cankers—cytospora in particular—are common), cutting it out along with some healthy growth for insurance.

MULTIPLE TRUNKS

Many deciduous and evergreen shrubs can have single or multiple trunks and their proper development is important to the overall shape and vigor of the plant. The color, texture, and line of a trunk are especially important in cold-weather climates where the winter garden is mostly barren. A well-shaped trunk or a cluster of sinuous trunks can provide a much-needed focal point at that time.

Shrubs with a typical trunk—fairly small like the deciduous star magnolia (*Magnolia stellata*)—often grow with properly attached branches. If an occasional shoot grows with a narrow angle of attachment, bend, spread, or weight the supple shoot just as you would with any ornamental or edible tree.

If you want to convert a shrub with a single trunk to one with multiple trunks, you should prune in spring. When planting bare-root container or balled-and-burlapped stock in the spring, deciduous and evergreen shrubs can be cut back severely to stimulate lots of new shoots. Cut to less than 12" above the soil on the trunk if you want new trunks near the soil. (On grafted trees, make sure *not* to cut below the graft union or you'll lose the cultivar.) If more shoots arise than you need, rub off the tender new shoots before they reach 6" long. Another option is to let everything grow unrestrained until mid to late summer and eliminate the undesirable trunks with late-season pruning.

DECIDUOUS SHRUBS

New or established deciduous shrubs can be pruned in different seasons to help the plant grow evenly or correct lopsided growth. In spring, prune the vigorous-growing side of a misshapen plant *lightly* and the slow-growing side *heavily,* or *harder.* Remember, spring pruning promotes branching and, to a lesser degree, growth. The more you prune, the more branching and growth you'll induce.

Try to spread corrective pruning over the spring and summer. Head back the weaker growth with some severity in spring to bring about more new shoots, but leave the vigorous limbs unpruned. In summer, make thinning cuts to remove unwanted growth on the larger portion of the foliage. After several seasons of this special attention, the foliage will look more uniform and well balanced.

To improve the shape of a shrub, head back branches heavily in spring to encourage new growth. To limit new growth, thin back long, crowded, or unneeded branches lightly.

NO PRUNING REQUIRED

Some deciduous shrubs are so well behaved they seldom need pruning, although removing damaged, diseased, and dead tissue is helpful.

Azaleas (*Rhododendron* spp.)

Barberries (*Berberis* spp.)

Bayberry (*Myrica pensylvanica*)

Beautyberry
   (*Callicarpa bodinieri giraldii*)

Buffaloberry, Silver
   (*Shepherdia argentea*)

Enkianthus (*Enkianthus* spp.)

Euonymus, Winged
   (*Euonymus alata*)

Flowering quince
   (*Chaenomeles speciosa*)*

Harry Lauder's Walking Stick
   (*Corylus avellana* 'Contorta')*

Lilac (*Syringa vulgaris*)*

Magnolia, Star (*Magnolia stellata*)

Maples: Fullmoon and **Japanese**
   (*Acer japonicum, A. palmatum*)

Pomegranate (*Punica granatum*)*

Privet, Common
   (*Ligustrum vulgare*) (as a shrub)

Redbuds (*Cercis* spp.)

Rose of Sharon (*Hibiscus syriacus*)

Serviceberries (*Amelanchier* spp.)*

Siberian pea shrub
   (*Caragana arborescens*)

Silverberry and Elaeagnus
   (*Elaeagnus commutata,*
   E. multiflora)

Sumacs (*Rhus* spp.)* (as a Shrub)

Tree peonies (*Paeonia* spp.)

Viburnums (*Viburnum* spp.)
   (shrubs)

Winter hazels (*Corylopsis* spp.)

Wintersweet (*Chimonanthus praecox*)

Witch hazels (*Hamamelis* spp.)

Plants marked with an (*) naturally grow as a small thicket of shoots and may need to be contained in their sideways expansion.

LATE SUMMER- OR FALL-FLOWERING SHOOTS: Deciduous shrubs that grow shoots all spring and blossom in late summer or fall are called late summer- or fall-flowering shoot shrubs. The flowers form only on new growth and bloom near the end of shoots. Once the flowers are spent, they will not rebloom again at the same location. If the shrub is left unpruned, the next bloom will occur on new growth at the end of the shoot.

Traditionally, late summer- or fall-flowering shrubs are pruned heavily in early spring before the leaves open. In mild-winter areas, you can prune in the fall if you want to deadhead the blossoms for winter. Pruning late summer- or fall-flowering shrubs usually means cutting back fairly severely to pairs of healthy buds near the ground, leaving them with very short, knobby trunks after pruning.

SHRUBS THAT NEED SEVERE PRUNING

Butterfly bushes (*Buddleia* spp.)
  (in warm-winter areas)
False spirea (*Sorbaria sorbifolia*)
Fuchsias (*Fuchsia* spp.)
  (in cold winter areas)
Honeysuckle, Southern bush
  (*Diervilla sessilifolia*)
Hydrangea, Bigleaf or Garden
  (*Hydrangea macrophylla*)*

Hydrangea, Peegee (*Hydrangea paniculata* var. *grandiflora*)
Kerria, Japanese (*Kerria japonica*)
Plumbago, Dwarf
  (*Ceratostigma plumbaginoides*)
Russian sages (*Perovskia* spp.)
Spice bush
  (*Calycanthus occidentalis*)*
  (in warm-winter areas)

(*) These shrubs are often left with a reduced branching structure after severe pruning and should have the trunk(s) pruned clean of branches for several feet above the ground.

FLOWERING ON SECOND-YEAR SHOOTS: Many deciduous shrubs grow shoots that flower only in the second season of their growth, usually in spring before new growth begins at the tip bud. These ornamental shrubs, like peach trees, don't flower again after the stem is two years old. Also, limb position is not important when it comes to encouraging flowering. Some of these shrubs, such as weeping forsythia (*Forsythia suspensa*), have a fountainlike habit, with vertical growth in the middle and cascading branches near the outer portion of the canopy. Left to their own, these shrubs will flower every spring on short growth that is farther from the middle of the plant and become more raggedy with every year.

Such plants need an annual trim to keep them from becoming too rangy. Use thinning cuts each spring after bloom to entirely remove shoots that have already flowered. This will give rise to new shoots that will flower the next spring. The goals are to maintain an evenly balanced shrub and remove all spent blooms to vigorous side-growth by cutting back to the most vigorous new shoots or buds below the flowers.

SECOND-YEAR-FLOWERING SHRUBS

Beauty bushes
  (*Kolkwitzia amabilis*)

Cream bush or Ocean spray
  (*Holodiscus discolor*)

Currant, Pink winter
  (*Ribes sanguineum*)

Deutzias (*Deutzia* spp.)

Forsythia, White
  (*Abeliophyllum distichum*)

Jasmines: Italian and **Winter**
  (*Jasminum humile, J. nudiflorum*)

Lilac
  (*Syringa microphylla, S. prestoniae*)
  (certain species)

Mock orange
  (*Philadelphus coronarius*)

Spirea, Bridal wreath and **Spirea**
  (*Spiraea prunifolia, S. thunbergii*)

Tamarisk, Spring-flowering
  (*Tamarix parviflora* or
  T. tetranda)

Weigelas (*Weigela* spp.)

Forsythia

BOTANICAL NAME: *Forsythia intermedia*

PLANT TYPE: Deciduous Shrub

SIZE: Grows to 6'–10' wide and to 10' tall on unpruned plants.

GROWING HABITS: Arching branches sometimes sprout from ground. Flowers on second-year shoots.

TIME TO PRUNE: Prune directly after blooming. Shearing in spring will destroy many of the second-year, flower-bearing shoots.

NEW SHOOTS AFTER CUTTING BARE STEMS? Doesn't apply as most cuts are thinning cuts near the ground.

SPECIAL PRUNING POINTERS: No pruning is ever required if the plant has enough room to grow and you

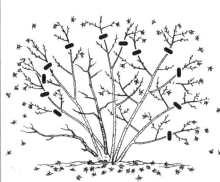

Before: After forsythia flowers have faded, cut back long, aged, or damaged branches at the base.

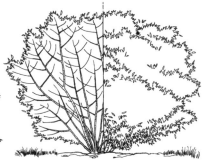

After: Vigorous new stems will arise to replace the stems that were removed.

Forsythia *(continued)*

don't mind some bare stems at the bottom of the shrub. Otherwise, cut one-fourth to one-third of the older shoots that have flowered to within 4" of the soil so the base of the plant doesn't get too dense.

STEP BY STEP: *1.* If new plant is well branched, plant without pruning.

2. Let bloom the second year, then prune up to one-fourth of the shoots with spent flowers to within 4" of the ground. *3.* After the second or third year, plants can have up to one-third of the two-year-old branches removed.

Common butterfly bush

BOTANICAL NAME: *Buddleia davidii*

PLANT TYPE: Deciduous Shrub

SIZE: Individual shoots grow from 3'–10' tall and the width is about half the height.

GROWING HABITS: Deciduous shrub in cold-winter areas (down to well below 0°F). Can be evergreen or partially evergreen in warm-winter climates. Long vertical growth arches over at the ends with the weight of the blossoms. Flowers are born on new growth in mid or late summer. Prone to rain and wind damage during and after bloom.

TIME TO PRUNE: In early or mid spring, cut back all shoots from last year to one-half to one-fourth their height. Leave any new healthy shoots—these will flower in midsummer or later. To prevent wind and rain damage, cut back long shoots when bloom is over or by early fall.

NEW SHOOTS AFTER CUTTING BARE STEMS? Will sprout from bare growth, but look for trace buds to be sure of the location of the sprout.

SPECIAL PRUNING POINTERS: Over time, the base of the shrub gets congested

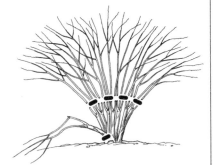

Before: In spring, cut back the previous growth to ¼ of its original height or about 6" above the ground. In cold climates, stems may die back to the ground and can be removed entirely.

After: Thin back overly long stems to a side branch and head back weak growth by ⅓ of its total length.

Common butterfly bush *(continued)*

with many old, thick stubs from cutting back in the spring. Use thinning cuts to take out some of the oldest limbs to make room for vigorous new growth. Be sure to rub off unwanted sprouts anytime you see them growing in the wrong place or in the wrong direction.

STEP BY STEP: *1.* Prune newly planted stock to within 6" of the ground.

2. Let shrub grow and bloom, then cut out any extra lanky or crowded shoots in late summer. *3.* In early to mid spring, cut back the previous year's growth to one or two buds. *4.* Head back growth that might be too floppy or weak to take the rain, wind, or snow by up to one-third in the early fall.

EVERGREEN SHRUBS

Evergreen shrubs have the advantage of always being in leaf, so it's easy to see the effects of your pruning. Beginners can prune with caution and see how much more light filters through the canopy with each careful snip. More confident pruners can proceed with abandon and quickly see the results at the end.

Although evergreens have foliage throughout the year, the activity of both the leaves and stem growth drops considerably in winter. Pruning during this time leaves the exposed cuts vulnerable to freezing (dieback) and should be avoided. When thinning the foliage, moderation is the best tactic. Increasing the amount of sunlight throughout the shrub's foliage helps promote a fuller canopy and healthy flower buds, but severe pruning allows too much direct sunlight onto the lower branches and trunk, sunburning the young bark.

There are two major types of large evergreen shrubs: broadleaf and conifers. Camellias (*Camellia* spp.), hollies (*Ilex* spp.), and rhododendrons and azaleas (*Rhododendron* spp.) are examples of broadleaf shrubs. The more compact or dwarf forms of firs (*Abies* spp.), junipers (*Juniperus* spp.), pines (*Pinus* spp.), and spruces (*Picea* spp.), are needle-leafed conifer shrubs.

BROADLEAF SHRUBS: Broadleaf evergreen shrubs come in many forms but they are distinguished from conifers by the absence of true needles. Most broadleaf evergreen shrubs form good branching and

BROADLEAF EVERGREEN SHRUBS THAT SPROUT NEW GROWTH FROM BARE STEMS

Barberry, Darwin
  (*Berberis darwinii*)

Boxwood, Common
  (*Buxus sempervirens*)

Camellia, Common
  (*Camellia japonica*)

Coffeeberry, California
  (*Rhamnus californica*)

Coyote brush
  (*Baccharis pilularis* 'Twin Peaks')

Escallonias (*Escallonia* spp.)

Euryops, Gray-leaved
  (*Euryops pectinatus*)
  (not very old limbs or trunk)

Firethorn (*Pyracantha coccinea*)

Heath, Biscay (*Erica mediterranea*)

Hollies: American and **Japanese**
  (*Ilex opaca, I. crenata*)

Laurel, English (*Prunus laurocerasus*)

Lavenders (*Lavandula* spp.)
  (to a point, limited effect)

Oak, Coast live (*Quercus agrifolia*)

Oleander (*Nerium oleander*)

Osmanthus, Holly-leaf
  (*Osomanthus heterophyllus*)

Pineapple guava (*Feijoa sellowiana*)

Pride of Madeira
  (*Echium fastuosum*)

Privet, Japanese
  (*Ligustrum japonicum*)

Sage, Jerusalem (*Phlomis fruticosa*)

Sage, Mexican bush
  (*Salvia leucantha*)

Sagebrush, California
  (*Artemisia californica*)

Sweet bay (*Laurus nobilis*)
  (the true spice)

Tobira (*Pittisporum tobira*)

flower buds regardless of the limb's position, so toothpicks and other spreading devices are seldom if ever required.

Some broadleaf evergreen shrubs naturally grow with multiple trunks, and you can prune the foliage to highlight the line of the trunks all the way to the ground. To achieve this effect you may want to begin at planting time by pruning back the multiple trunks to within 1' of the ground to stimulate more branching. Repeated summer shearing thereafter will encourage more side shoots and a bushier habit from the temporary loss of tip-bud dominance. If you are going to display the trunks, thin out unwanted shoots in summer, keeping the most aesthetically pleasing ones. Summer pruning is also a good time to permanently remove unwanted foliage so the trunks are easily seen.

Other broadleaf evergreens, like holly shrubs, are more naturally inclined to form a single trunk. To make a multi-trunk shrub, you must prune it back to near the ground in early spring, which will encourage a selection of shoots for you to choose from. Select the best-looking trunks, and then summer prune to remove the unwanted trunks.

To control leggy growth and encourage a bushy form, pinch or clip back the shrub's leader and any of the lateral shoots. Repeated shearing will make the shrub look more like a hedge or crudely shaped topiary, but shearing that is too frequent may eliminate flowering.

If the plant blooms in spring, prune it after the bloom is over. Summer-blooming plants can be clipped in the early spring before growth begins. In both cases, this pruning will act just like the dormant pruning of deciduous shrubs and stimulate multiple side shoots to bloom the next season. Leggy growth or flower heads that flop over in the rain, or from their own weight, can usually be corrected with a firm, but not severe, shearing after the flowers have faded. The more floppy the blossoming stems, the farther back you should cut.

When pruning any kind of evergreen shrub, cut back all growth to a side shoot or to the branch collar. To be safe, don't clip any farther back on a limb or shoot than you can see existing healthy green leaves, buds, or shoots. Many broadleaf evergreen shrubs will, however, make new growth from bare stems after determined pruning.

CONIFER SHRUBS: Evergreen conifer shrubs often grow with a natural, well-behaved, uniform shape without much help from the gardener. Each has a distinctive form: many small shrubby pines are nearly as wide as they are tall; dwarf spruces, such as the Colorado spruce (*Picea pungens* 'Fat Albert'), have a well-behaved pyramidal shape like a Christmas tree; most dwarf conifers form tight, compact growth; and while yews (*Taxus* spp.) are often used for very tightly sheared hedges and topiary, they form a decent, but somewhat frumpy, shrub. Their tidy habits don't mean conifers can't do with a little clipping from a fastidious gardener.

To make a conifer's growth more dense, clip its "candles"— the lengthy buds that look like fuzzy candles with no wick. Pinching or clipping back one-half of the candle causes side shoots and denser foliage. This is easy on most coniferous shrubs, but time-consuming on tree-sized conifers. (Do not clip back the highest candle on the leader or tip of the trunk unless you want to reduce or stop the shrub's height.) Coniferous shrubs make new growth only where there's foliage, so don't cut back into old, bare shoots, branches, or limbs (exceptions are yews and redwood trees [*Sequoia* spp.]).

Conifers with a fairly compact foliage are usually pruned with hedge shears in late spring in cold-winter areas (after the possibility of a hard frost in *any* climate) and once or twice in the summer if subsequent growth gets rangy. Where winters come on hard and cold, refrain from shearing conifers after early August. This will give any growth from the most recent shearing a chance to "harden off" for winter.

Keep other plants near dwarf conifers well pruned as any overlapping foliage causes shade that may bring about foliage dieback at the base of the conifers. Once the foliage is dead, there will be a permanent hole in the foliage.

Corrective pruning of wayward limbs should be carried out

When shearing conifers, attempt to prune off the "candles," or tips of the branches.

like you would with any deciduous shrub; head back lengthy growth to a well-placed side shoot, dormant bud, or trace bud. Crowded limbs should be thinned out, but be sure to leave the branch collar to allow for a healthy callus. (Most conifers don't have a noticeable branch bark ridge, but they do have a pronounced branch collar.)

Firethorn, Pyracantha

BOTANICAL NAMES: *Pyracantha coccinea, P. fortuneana*

PLANT TYPE: Evergreen Shrub (Broadleaf)

SIZE: Can sprawl in all directions to 8'–15' tall and wide, depending upon the species. Trained to a trellis or wall, it may grow to 20' tall or wide.

GROWING HABITS: Bears flowers (and colorful berries) on spurs formed on one-year-old growth.

TIME TO PRUNE: Prune out any dead and blackened limbs whenever they are seen, as this may be fire blight. Prune in spring and summer to control tendency to produce long shoots. Use thinning cuts for the most control.

NOTE: Fire blight is a nasty disease that can be transmitted by your pruning shears. With all visibly damaged growth, cut off at least 12", preferably 18", past the visible damage into clean,

Firethorn, Pyracantha *(continued)*

green growth nearer the heart of the shrub. Be sure to cleanse your pruning shear's blade *after each cut* with 10% bleach-and-water solution, 100% Lysol™, or 100% rubbing alcohol.

NEW SHOOTS AFTER CUTTING BARE STEMS? Sprouts from bare stems. Look for trace buds to ascertain where the new shoot will form.

SPECIAL PRUNING POINTERS: Pyracanthas are vigorous growers— both spring and summer pruning are helpful to keep the foliage under control. Summer pruning of the current season's growth will help form more flower spurs and, subsequently, more berries. Pyracanthas can be trained to almost any form—shrub, espalier, topiary, or single-trunk small tree. As an espalier, a pyracantha requires some summer pruning of new growth to form spurs and to keep its foliage in bounds.

NOTE: Pyracantha has nasty, dull thorns that can be quite painful and puncture wounds may fester. Use leather gloves and a long-sleeved shirt to protect against thorns.

STEP BY STEP: 1. In midsummer, cut back all shoots to three to five side leaves or buds. *2.* Later in summer, cut farther back to two or three leaves. *3.* One month or more before the first freeze, thin out any unwanted shoots and cut back to fat flower buds on base of other shoots—these will flower next spring.

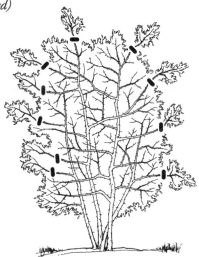

Before: To form flower spurs, cut back long side shoots to 3 to 5 buds in early summer, and again, to 2 to 3 buds, in late summer. Use heading cuts where necessary to fill gaps.

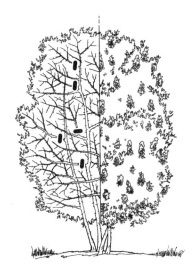

After: In early fall, thin out unwanted growth.

Lavender (English, French, Spanish, and many cultivars)

BOTANICAL NAMES: *Lavandula angusti-folia, L. dentata, L. Stoechas*

PLANT TYPE: Evergreen Shrub (Broadleaf)

SIZE: Small shrubs grow to 8"–36" tall and equally wide, depending upon species and variety.

GROWING HABITS: Evergreen foliage, if left unpruned, grows from the tips of last year's growth. Some branch without pruning, but it often doesn't make enough short, well-branched growth to prevent a leggy, floppy plant. For a compact plant that can hold the heavy flower stalks up, especially in rainy weather, a yearly shearing is required. Unpruned plants develop bare bases and tops flop over when sprinkled or rained on.

TIME TO PRUNE: In cold climates, prune back spent flower stalks and up to 2" of last year's growth in mid spring—after the risk of hard freezing has past. (Leaving the somewhat ugly dead flower stems and the foliage uncut for the winter may help protect against severe freezing and dry, cold winds.) In mild climates (coastal California and southern coastal states), the flowers and foliage can be trimmed after blooming to promote a healthy, dense foliage by fall. (These plants look presentable during the winter.)

NEW SHOOTS AFTER CUTTING BARE STEMS? Cautious pruners don't cut back into bare lavender stems. Severe pruning into bare growth will often stimulate new growth, but there is a small chance the plant will die. Severe pruning should be done months before the danger of the first frost, so the new growth has time to toughen up before winter. Severe pruning is best done only as a last resort, even in very mild climates.

SPECIAL PRUNING POINTERS: Don't be afraid to shear lavenders back solidly. A light trimming will only encourage the flower stalks and even the foliage to fall over in the rain or wind, or when sprinkled.

Before: When spring weather becomes mild in cold climates, remove any winter-killed stems. In warm climates, shear the plant back after blooming.

After: After flowering, pinch back lanky shoots. The plant may fare better in cold-winter climates if the old flower stems remain.

Lavender *(continued)*

STEP BY STEP: *1.* Look for the small buds of the new leaves along the stems. *2.* Cut back severely after bloom is over, but leave some of the stems with visible new growth. *3.* During the season, pinch back or clip any wayward shoots that grow well above the rest of the foliage.

Mugho pine

BOTANICAL NAME: *Pinus mugo*

PLANT TYPE: Evergreen Shrub (Conifer)

SIZE: Grows slowly to 4'.

GROWING HABITS: Like many dwarf conifers, often naturally grows as a dense symmetrical shrub.

TIME TO PRUNE: As the new shoots (called candles) begin to grow in the spring, and needles begin to lengthen.

NEW SHOOTS AFTER CUTTING BARE STEMS? Will not make new shoots if cut back to bare wood.

SPECIAL PRUNING POINTERS: Avoid pruning or shearing needles as the tips will turn brown.

STEP BY STEP: 1. Purchase a well-formed plant and you'll avoid the need to prune after planting. 2. Any awkward limbs that protrude above the overall shape of the shrub should be cut back to a well-placed side shoot with a thinning cut in spring or summer. 3. To make the foliage more dense, simply pinch or cut back the candles each spring by one-third to one-half or more.

TREES

Choosing the correct trees for your landscape is one of the most important and enjoyable decisions for the gardener. Very few forms of plant life inspire and awe us like trees: they temper their surroundings with a sense of scale; they provide much needed shade and shelter to people, animals, plants, and surrounding buildings; they connect plant life lesser in size by defining borders, softening edges, and punctuating lawns.

Trees come in all sizes, shapes, colors, and growing habits. Many deciduous trees signify spring with their new green growth and lull you into fall with brilliant foliage changing to reds, oranges, and browns before they drop off and leave the magnificent tree scaffold barren, but nonetheless impressive.

Evergreen trees have a diverse range of leaves and needles that gives them a more solid year-round presence in the landscape. While deciduous trees may offer more botanical flash with their seasonal beauty, evergreen trees are extremely effective structural elements, perfect for framing a garden or yard. They can be tricky to prune—because they always have foliage, their branch structure is usually hidden—but their "stability" is less worrisome.

Tree pruning is infinitely easier if the correct tree is chosen for the correct place; if you are constantly battling against a tree's natural desire to grow taller or wider, pruning loses its luster, and in the process of trying to control the tree's growth, you may permanently damage it.

DECIDUOUS TREES

During the summer, much of the countryside is gently concealed with a patina of green from the leaves cloaking deciduous native trees. A brilliant blaze of fall color draws attention to the tree's foliage. As the spent leaves of all colors from hot yellow and dull orange to muddy brown settle to the forest floor, the tree's branch structure is slowly unveiled. Then, fluffy snow outlines the sinuous and angular forms of each branch in winter.

DECIDUOUS TREES REQUIRING LITTLE OR NO PRUNING

Angelica trees (*Aralia* spp.)

Buckeye, Bottlebrush
  (*Aesculus parviflora*)

Cherry, Cornelian (*Cornus mas*)

Chinese Flame tree
  (*Koelreuteria bipinnata*)

Cotoneaster, Many-flowered
  (*Cotoneaster multiflorus*)

Dogwood, Flowering
  (*Cornus florida*)

Dogwood, Korean (*C. kousa*)

Goldenrain tree
  (*Koelreuteria paniculata*)

Goumi (*Elaeagnus multiflora*)

Maple, Norway (*Acer platanoides*)

Maple, Red (*A. rubrum*)

Maple, Sugar (*A. saccharum*)

Olive, Russian
  (*Elaeagnus angustifolia*)

Persimmons (*Diospyros* spp.)

Redbud, Eastern (*Cercis canadensis*)

Redbud, Western
  (*C. occidentalis*)

Siberian pea shrub
  (*Caragana arborescens*)

Snowdrop tree or **Carolina Silver-bell** (*Halesia carolina*)

Sumac, Staghorn (*Rhus typhina*)

Deciduous trees can provide accents of color and form, stunning backdrops, and seasonal delights in the home garden. And gardeners can choose from a staggering array of exotic (non-native) deciduous trees that, compared to native trees, often have richer-colored foliage. Still others provide unique branching patterns or bark textures, but all can be improved structurally and aesthetically with an occasional judicious pruning to improve their appearance.

As you do with most plants, try to select trees that require little or no pruning at first. If you can fill in the larger areas of the garden with big trees that grow without the guidance of the pruner's blade, you'll have more time to pamper the smaller plants closer to the house. Talk to the Cooperative Extension Service in your area, or local arborists, landscapers, landscape architects, or nurseryfolks about the best care-free trees for your area.

BASIC DECIDUOUS TREE SHAPES: Nature has assigned each tree a predetermined shape. While the edges of the crown may vary and there will always be individual exceptions, genetics control the overall form. Prune in a way that enhances the inherent shape or pattern of each different tree. For example, the quaking aspen (*Populus tremuloides*) naturally grows as a tall, narrow column. Keeping the tree down to a

---

DECIDUOUS TREES WITH ROUND SHAPES

Apples and **Crab apples**
  (*Malus* spp.)
Birch, Sweet or Cherry
  (*Betula lenta*)
Buckeyes, California and **Red**
  (*Aesculus californica, A. pavia*)
Catalpa, Southern
  (*Catalpa bignonioides*)
Cherry, Japanese flowering
  (*Prunus serrula*)
Dogwoods: Flowering and **Giant**
  (*Cornus controversa, C. florida*)
Elm, Chinese (*Ulmus parvifolia*)
Honey locust, Common
  (*Gleditsia triacanthos*)
Hornbeams: American and
  Common (*Carpinus betulus,*
  C. caroliniana)
Magnolia, Saucer
  (*Magnolia* × *soulangiena*)
Maples: Black (*Acer nigrum*)
  Coliseum (*A. cappadocicum*)
  Fullmoon (*A. japonicum*)
  Hedge (*A. campestre*)

Italian (*A. opalus*)
Japanese (*A. palmatum*)
Red (*A. rubrum*)
  Trident (*A. buergeranum*)
Mulberries, Black and **Red**
  (*Morus nigra, M. rubra*)
Oaks: Black (*Quercus kelloggii*)
  Bur (*Q. macrocarpa*)
  Chestnut (*Q. montana*)
  Post (*Q. stellata*)
  Valley (*Q. lobata*)
  White (*Q. alba*)
Pawpaw (*Asimina triloba*)
Pecan (*Carya illinoinensis*)
Persimmons: American and
  Chinese (*Diospyros virginiana,*
  D. kaki)
Redbud: Eastern (*Cercis candensis*),
  Judas tree (*C. siliquastrum*)
Serviceberries or **Amelanchier**
  trees (*Amelanchier* spp.)
Sumacs: Shiny and **Staghorn**
  (*Rhus copallina, R. typhina*)
Walnuts (*Juglans* spp.)

squat, wide shape can be done—but only with *considerable* effort and the possibility of harming the tree. Pruning as a reflection of Nature keeps trees looking natural, doesn't cause permanent damage like topping, and requires the least exertion. Tree shapes are not precise like architectural forms, but there is a range of shapes, and a diversity of names for the same basic shape. It is not easy to classify tree canopy names, and each reference book has a slightly different rationale for each definition.

Japanese maples and black maples have round tree crowns.

ROUND TREE SHAPES: Trees with roundish crowns are also referred to as globular or mounded. These terms refer to the mature shape, which ranges from nearly round to more broad than tall, to a mushroom caplike outline. In simple terms, these trees don't have a narrow, vertical, or triangular form to their foliage. They have what arborists call a decurrent growth pattern, or many codominant shoots.

PYRAMIDAL TREE SHAPES: This form is also called conical, triangular, or columnar. Trees with this crown shape range from a traditional Christmas tree (conifers in general are more likely to have this shape) to a boxy-wide, columnar, but not narrow, shape. When mature, some pyramidal-shaped trees may become more like the round shape mentioned earlier. Some trees start out displaying excurrent growth patterns and some actually evolve into a decurrent form as they mature into a rounded crown.

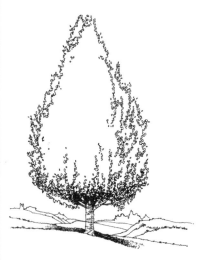

Pin oaks and birches are good examples of pyramidal tree crowns.

VERTICAL TREE SHAPES: The vertical crown (also called columnar) is proportionally taller than it is wide. Most deciduous trees do not display the same narrow habit as some of the vertical evergreen conifers. Again, when mature, some of the trees may have a roundish crown. Like pyramidal trees, young vertical-shaped trees are usually excurrent at first and the older trees, with their round crowns, have become decurrent.

NATURAL DECIDUOUS BRANCHING PATTERNS: Without much regard to shape, all trees have a limited number of options for how their limbs grow. The branching pattern is built into its genes, so if a narrow angle of attachment is intrinsic to a tree's branches, you would have to spend a lot of time correcting this tendency. If the growth pattern is common to most of the branches, chances are the tree has evolved sturdy tissues that compensate for the narrow angles. Furthermore, trying to change the natural pattern of branching can lead to disease and rot. If you are considering changing the natural shape or branch pattern of a tree, you've probably got the wrong tree for the spot. (If you still want to manipulate the tree's branches, begin when the tree is young—immediately after planting. Stop all shaping *as soon as possible* because pruning the major branches later in the tree's life will promote disease and rot.)

Quaking aspens and upright junipers are good examples of vertical tree crowns—from base to tip.

DECIDUOUS TREE SCAFFOLD SHAPES: As a gardener, you're not always willing to follow exactly in the footsteps of Nature. There are pruning options for deciduous trees that deviate slightly from the natural patterns. They tend to get rather large, so any pruning should be done in the first five years to shape the primary scaffold. These basic cuts can only be done while the tree is quite young; otherwise, the pruning will have the same effect as topping—allowing disease and rot to enter its core.

CENTRAL LEADER SHAPE WITH EXCURRENT TREES: When purchasing a well-formed tree in any climate, look for an excurrent tree with a straight, well-defined central leader. If there are two vertical leaders

DECIDUOUS TREES WITH VERTICAL SHAPES

Aspen, Quaking
  (*Populus tremuloides*)

Birches: River and **Gray**
  (*Betula nigra, B. populifolia*)

Cherry, Black
  (*Prunus serotina*)*

Crab apple, Flowering
  (*Malus 'Red Baron'*)

Locust, Black
  (*Robinia pseudoacacia*)*

Oak, Skyrocket
  (*Quercus robur* 'Fastigiata')

Pear, Flowering
  (*Pyrus calleryana* 'Chanticleer')

Willow, Pussy
  (*Salix discolor*)

DECIDUOUS TREES WITH PYRAMIDAL SHAPES

Alders (*Alnus* spp.) (all)
Ashes (*Fraxinus* spp.) (all)
Bald cypress (*Taxodium distichum*)
Birches (*Betula* spp.) (most)
Box elder (*Acer negundo*)*
Catalpa, Western or **Northern**
  (*Catalpa speciosa*)
Crab apples (*Malus tschonoskii,*
  M. yunnanensis)*
Elms: Chinese and **Japanese**
  (*Ulmus parvifolia, U. japonica*)*
Hackberry (*Celtis occidentalis*)*
Hollies (*Ilex* spp.) (most)
Lindens: American and **Common**
  (*Tilia americana, T. × europaea*)*
Locust, Black
  (*Robinia pseudoacacia*)*
Maples: Bigleaf or **Oregon**
  (*Acer macrophyllum*)
  David's (*A. davidii*)

Hornbeam (*A. carpinifolium*)
Japanese snakebark
  (*A. capillipes*)
  Paperbark (*A. griseum*)
  Red (*A. rubrum*)
  Sugar (*A. sacharum*)
  Vine (*A. circinatum*)(all maples)*
Oak, Pin (*Quercus palustris*)
  (when young)
Pear, Ornamental Bradford
  (*Pyrus calleryana*)
Pears, Edible (*P. communis*)
  (European)
Redwood, Dawn
  (*Metasequoia glyptostroboides*)
Sweet gum, American
  (*Liquidambar styraciflua*)
Sycamores (*Platanus* spp.)* (all)
Tulip tree (*Liriodendron tulipifera*)
Tupelo, Black (*Nyssa sylvatica*)

*Denotes trees that evolve into round-shaped canopies.

(codominant stems) they'll be competitive, so be sure one is clipped off
to make a single leader. When one is gone, the retained leader will grow
faster. Another option is clipping the weaker codominant off or reduc-

ing its size by one-third and keeping the healthiest leader to encourage a taller, faster-growing tree. If you want to slightly dwarf the tree, keep the smaller of the two leaders.

Second, look for well-placed branches. They should be evenly spaced both around the circumference and along the height of the trunk—about every 12"–24" along the trunk. The angle of attachment should be what is typical for the particular species you're considering. The importance of a good leader and properly placed branches is why you should select a tree at a local nursery rather than buying one from a mail-order company.

Pruning a deciduous excurrent ornamental tree is done much in the same way as central leader fruit trees. If all the branches are well balanced on the bare-root, balled-and-burlapped, or container tree you've chosen, there's no reason to prune anything at planting time. (Remember, the tip buds send a chemical signal that initiates root-hair growth *before* the new leaves appear.) Otherwise, clip the leader back if you want to invigorate side shoots. Make sure that the first bud below your cut on the leader sprouts vertically to become the new leader, or what is called a modified central leader tree on fruit trees. If the first shoot doesn't begin to grow vertically, tie a stick to the existing leader and attach the wayward shoot to the stick to train its growth vertically.

If all the new shoots below the new leader grow at a narrow angle of attachment, cut the leader below the longest shoots after the tree is in leaf to stimulate new shoots with wider angles of attachment. Another alternative is to spread the young shoots with toothpicks or clothespins to a normal angle for the particular type of tree. Once you've established which shoots to grow, head back any shoots that are too long, too vertical, or not branched well enough. The heading cuts will bring about more side shoots on each branch.

Let all sprouts grow unencumbered the first summer, if possible. The one important exception is to make sure no other shoot grows taller than the central leader. Firmly head back any competing shoot so the central leader's tip bud remains dominant and be sure to remove any suckers from the root system as soon as you see them.

In the second year, branches often need heading cuts in the spring to stimulate side-branching. During the second summer, continue to

BRANCHING PATTERNS

The natural angle of attachment for various deciduous trees can grow in either the excurrent or decurrent pattern, depending on the age and their genetics.

NARROW-ANGLED, UPRIGHT ATTACHMENT

Narrow-angled branch attachments range from almost vertical to nearly 45° angles. These trees are often classified as decurrent.

Maples: Mountain (*Acer spicatum*)
　Striped (*A. pensylvanicum*)
Pawpaw (*Asimina triloba*)
Poplar, Eastern
　(*Populus deltoides*)
Willow, Pussy
　(*Salix discolor*)

FORTY-FIVE DEGREE ATTACHMENT

This is the ideal angle of attachment for deciduous fruit trees. Many of these trees are decurrent.

Birches: River (*Betula nigra*)
　Sweet (*B. lenta*)
　Yellow (*B. lutea*)
Cherry, Black
　(*Prunus Serotina*)
Hickory, Shagbark
　(*Carya ovata*)
Locust, Black
　(*Robinia pseudoacacia*)
Maples: Black (*Acer nigrum*)
　Red (*A. rubrum*)
　Silver (*A. saccharinum*)
　Sugar (*A. saccharum*)
Oaks: Black and **Scarlet** (*Quercus velutina, Q. coccinea*)

Pecan (*Carya illinoinensis*)
Sweet gum, American
　(*Liquidambar styraciflua*)
Tulip tree (*Liriodendron tulipifera*)
Walnuts: Butternut and **Eastern**
　black (*Juglans cinerea, J. nigra*)
Willow, Black (*Salix nigra*)

NINETY-DEGREE HORIZONTAL ATTACHMENT

These trees will display either decurrent or excurrent patterns when young, often changing to mostly decurrent with age.

Beech, American
　(*Fagus grandifolia*)
Oaks: Bur (*Quercus macrocarpa*)
　Post (*Q. stellata*)
　White (*Q. alba*)
Plum, American (*Prunus americana*)
Sycamore, American planetree
　(*Platanus occidentalis*)
Tupelo, Black (*Nyssa sylvatica*)

BELOW HORIZONTAL, DESCENDING ATTACHMENT

This trait is more common to evergreen tree varieties than deciduous trees. These deciduous examples are decurrent.

Oaks: Swamp(*Quercus ellipsoidalis*)
　Northern pin (*Q. palustris*)
　Shingle (*Q. imbricaria*)
Willow, Weeping (*Salix babylonica*)

remove any root suckers and control any shoots or watersprouts competing with the leader's tip bud. During your summer pruning season, thin out any badly placed or odd-growing new laterals. Look for limbs that are out of position for the natural shape of the type of tree you're growing and remove them with thinning cuts. The second year is also the time to begin selecting the primary scaffold, so use thinning cuts to remove unwanted growth. Continue with the same pruning methods for another two or three years until it's difficult to reach the top of the leader.

CENTRAL LEADER SHAPE WITH DECURRENT TREES: A decurrent tree can be trained like a central leader tree, but it's seldom done. Use heading cuts to control the width of the tree and then select one superior central leader by using thinning cuts to remove competing leaders. Remember, these trees have many codominant shoots, branches, or limbs, so plenty of pruning will be required to select one main leader.

OPEN-CENTER AND DELAYED OPEN-CENTER SHAPES WITH EXCURRENT TREES: Open-center trees have their central leader cut out at planting time to force numerous side shoots that will become the primary scaffold. A delayed open-center tree is allowed to grow a central leader for three to five years as the primary scaffold is trained, then the leader is eventually removed. Other than treatment of the central leader, the pruning techniques are about the same for both open-center and delayed open-center trees.

Train delayed open-center trees just like central leader trees for the first three to five years. The leader is regrown each year so that when it's cut back new laterals will be generated. This develops a sturdy, well-placed primary scaffold with limbs 12"–24" apart vertically. After the main branches have been formed, the leader is permanently removed during summer using a thinning cut to control the tree's height.

In the early years of pruning both shapes, all branches must be cut back to a bud on the underside of the shoot that faces away from the middle. Choose a bud that is facing toward an open area in the crown to make the best use of space.

Excurrent ornamental trees can also be pruned to the open-center and delayed open-center form, but it's seldom done. Nonetheless, if you must control the height of excurrent ornamental trees, use a mixture of heading cuts and thinning cuts. The most significant reduction in height will be achieved with thinning cuts in summer. The open-center form will require more pruning throughout the year to control the excurrent tree's vertical tendencies.

OPEN-CENTER AND DELAYED OPEN-CENTER SHAPES FOR DECURRENT TREES: Decurrent trees are sometimes trained to open-center and delayed open-center forms to make them shorter and wider. This usually occurs when the wrong tree was planted in the wrong place. Rely heavily on thinning cuts to remove the unwanted vertical growth each summer. Some heading cuts that favor the wider or more horizontal shoots may be required. Here, summer heading cuts should be made to favor better-placed shoots or branches.

STANDARD SHAPE FOR DECURRENT AND EXCURRENT TREES: To achieve the standard shape on both decurrent and excurrent trees, train them in any of the above forms for a number of years. Leave all lower limbs uncut until the tree has developed branches well above 5'–8' to foster a stronger trunk. Then, use summer thinning cuts to remove all limbs from the ground to the desired height—leaving the lowest limbs high enough so it's possible to walk beneath the crown. You can begin removing a few of the lowest limbs in the second year, but the trunk will not develop its girth as rapidly. Since the tree may live for more than a hundred years, waiting to thin the side limbs for five years is a relatively small compromise.

Pin oak

BOTANICAL NAME: *Quercus palustris*

PLANT TYPE: Deciduous Tree

SIZE: Up to 50'–100' tall and about one-half as wide. Pyramidal-shaped when young and broad conical-shaped when mature.

GROWING HABITS: Medium to fast growth. Popular as a lawn or shade tree because it develops such a refined shape with almost no pruning. With age, the lower branches tend to droop to the ground.

TIME TO PRUNE: Spring heading will stimulate branching, but is seldom needed. Remove winter storm damage only enough to clean up the ground. Wait until spring pruning to make the final cuts to the branch collar. Prune any spring or summer storm damage as it occurs.

NEW SHOOTS AFTER CUTTING BARE STEMS? Too much risk that the stub will die and be an entry point for disease and rot.

Pin oak *(continued)*

SPECIAL PRUNING POINTERS: This oak tree has a tendency to grow two competing leaders or codominant shoots. As soon as you spot this problem, clip out one of the shoots. Leave the one with a strong center of attachment that appears more vigorous.

STEP BY STEP: *1.* After planting, only trim off damaged or completely misplaced shoots or limbs. Leave as many laterals and branches as possible to help build up the tree's trunk. *2.* Make sure the central leader stays higher than any other growth while the tree is young. Heading cuts in the spring will fill in any holes in the crown. *3.* As tree grows, remove any suckers. Thin out any poorly placed shoots or damaged branches. Use heading cuts to make laterals where they are needed—best done with young trees. *4.* As the tree matures, there is no reason to cut off the lower swooping branches. If you want to use the area under the canopy or attempt to have a lawn or ground cover (both problematic), use summer pruning to remove the lower limbs up to a comfortable level.

Before: When young, thin back competing leaders, cut back branches that cross and rub or compete for light, and remove root suckers and damaged branches as you see them.

After: Once mature, pin oaks need little pruning. Avoid late spring and summer pruning, and sterilize pruning shears where oak wilt is a problem.

Crab apple tree

BOTANICAL NAME: *Malus* spp.

PLANT TYPE: Deciduous Tree

SIZE: Many different sizes from 15' tall and 10' wide to 25' × 15'. Size depends upon the variety of crab apple and the origin of rootstock.

GROWING HABITS: Commonly grows as a central leader. Seldom needs yearly pruning if disease-free. Flowers on spurs formed on two-year-old branches. Can be shaped to any form used for fruiting apple and pear trees—standard, delayed open-center, open-center, dwarf central leader, or any of the many espalier forms.

TIME TO PRUNE: Like fruit trees, spring heading cuts are used to encourage laterals and branches. Spring and summer pruning are used to remove any damaged or diseased shoots, branches, or limbs. Natural cascading of the shoots tends to form plenty of bloom without pruning.

NEW SHOOTS AFTER CUTTING BARE STEMS? Sprouts readily from bare shoots, stems, branches, and limbs.

SPECIAL PRUNING POINTERS: Water-sprouts and suckers are especially troublesome with crab apple trees. Be sure to eliminate them with thinning cuts as soon as they're noticed. Be watchful for fire blight spreading down the shoot or limb. Cut back visibly damaged branches 12"–18" into healthy-looking growth. Sterilize pruners *after each cut* with a 10% bleach-and-water solution, 100% Lysol™, or 100% rubbing alcohol.

STEP BY STEP: *1.* After planting, cut leader only if you want an open-center or delayed open-center shape. Clip as few shoots or branches as necessary for a healthy form. *2.* By early summer, tie up the first shoot below the cut leader if you want a delayed open-center tree. Spread or tie down any vertical shoots for a wider tree. *3.* In summer, remove any crossing shoots. Use thinning cuts to let more light into the crown or to remove water-sprouts. Always remove suckers as soon as possible. When the tree reaches desired height, cut out the leader with a summer thinning cut.

Before: In early summer, use spreaders to push upright-growing shoots into 45° branching angles.

After: When shoots have become woody and adopt the proper branch angle, you can remove the spreaders.

EVERGREEN TREES

Evergreen foliage comes in a wide range of shapes: long, lacy needle-like leaves; stiff broad leaves with sharp points; squat, squarish needles; soft-textured round leaves; and even green stems full of chlorophyll with very few, tiny, lobed leaflets. Evergreen trees are easily divided into two categories: broadleaf and coniferous (with needles). And the leaves come in almost as many colors as cars: dark, rich green; bright chartreuse; regal silver-gray; frosty, glaucous blue; translucent lemon-yellow-green; and glossy, mirrorlike dark green.

Cold-winter climates limit the gardener's choices of evergreen trees. There are more possibilities for gardeners in warm-weather climates, and an even larger choice of evergreen trees for those in subtropical portions of the southern parts of the country—most tropical plants are evergreen.

EVERGREEN TREES REQUIRING LITTLE OR NO PRUNING

Once established, these trees need almost no pruning except for removing dead and diseased growth.

Cedars (*Cedrus* spp.) (all)
Cypresses, False and **True**
  (*Chamaecyparis* spp.,
  Cupressus spp.)
Douglas fir (*Pseudotsuga menziesii*)
Fern pine (*Podocarpus gracilior*)
Firs (*Abies* spp.) (all)
Hemlocks (*Tsuga* spp.) (all)
Magnolia, Southern or **Evergreen**
  (*Magnolia grandiflora*)

Maple (*Acer paxii*)
Pines (*Pinus* spp.) (all)
Redwood, Coastal
  (*Sequoia sempervirens*)
Sequoia, Giant
  (*Sequoiadendron giganteum*)
Totara
  (*Podocarpus totara*)
Yews (*Taxus* spp.) (all)

Regardless of where evergreen trees are grown, the pruning techniques are the same—although the season of pruning may vary. To begin, choose evergreens that need little attention from the clippers. Keep in mind that all full-sized conifer trees need plenty of room to grow naturally without much pruning. As with any plant, be sure to prune out the occasional limb that grows at an odd angle, trim growth

EVERGREEN TREE SHAPES

ROUND SHAPES

Cypress, Monterey
  (*Cupressus macrocarpa*) (narrow)
English laurel (*Prunus laurocerasus*)
Juniper, Alligator
  (*Juniperus deppeana pachyphlaea*)
Magnolia, Southern
  (*Magnolia grandiflora*)
Oak, Live (*Quercus agrifolia* and
  Q. virginiana)
Photinias (*Photinia davidiana*,
  P. × *fraseri*, *P. serratifolia*)
Pines: Chinese (*Pinus tabuliformis*)
  Montezuma (*P. montezumae*)
  Pitch (*P. rigida*)

PYRAMIDAL SHAPES

Arborvitae, American or
  Northern white cedar
  (*Thuja occidentalis*)
Cedar: Eastern red
  (*Juniperus virginiana*)
  Japanese (*Cryptomeria japonica*)
  Western red (*Thuja plicata*)
Cypress, Smooth Arizona
  (*Cupressus glabra*) (narrow)
Douglas fir
  (*Pseudotsuga menziesii*)
Firs: Balsam (*Abies balsamea*)
  White (*A. concolor*)
  Noble (*A. procera*)
  Spanish (*A. pinsapo*)
Hemlock: Eastern or **Canadian**
  (*Tsuga canadensis*)
  Western (*T. heterophylla*)
  (narrow)

Juniper, Chinese
  (*Juniperus chinensis*) (narrow)
Larch, European (*Larix decidua*)
Larch, Western
  (*L. occidentalis*) (narrow)
Nutmeg, California
  (*Torreya californica*)
Pines: Bishop (*Pinus muricata*)
  Japanese red pine
  (*P. densiflora*)
  Monterey (*P. muricata*)
  Ponderosa (*P. ponderosa*)
  Red (*P. resinosa*)
Redwood, Coastal
  (*Sequoia sempervirens*) (narrow)
Sequoia, Giant
  (*Sequoiadendron giganteum*)
  (narrow)
Spruce: Black (*Picea mariana*)
  Colorado (*P. pungens*)
  Norway (*P. abies*)
  White (*P. glauca*)
Yew, Common
  (*Taxus baccata*)

VERTICAL SHAPES

Cedar, Incense
  (*Calocedrus decurrens*)
Cypresses: Italian and **Leyland**
  (× *Cupressocyparis leylandii*,
  cupressus sempervirens),
  Cypress, White
  (*Chamaecyparis thyoides*)
  Lawson's Port Orford cedar
  (*C. lawsoniana*)
Juniper, Eastern red
  (*Juniperus virginiana*)

that detracts from the overall shape, remove damaged or diseased branches, and make sure no other limbs compete with the tip of the central leader.

BASIC EVERGREEN TREE SHAPES: Think of the mature crown as a silhouette that will be your template for pruning the tree. Similar to deciduous trees, you can train evergreens into whatever shape you want if you spend enough time and energy—bonsai trees are a good example. Be sure to ask your local nurseryperson about the shape for each tree you buy.

BASIC EVERGREEN BRANCHING PATTERNS

NARROW-ANGLED, UPRIGHT ATTACHMENT

Cypress, Italian
(*Cupressocyparis sempervirens*)
Yew, Irish
(*Taxus baccata* 'Stricta')

NINETY-DEGREE HORIZONTAL ATTACHMENT

Cedar, Eastern red
(*Juniperus virginiana*)
Cypress, Common bald
(*Taxodium distichum*)
Douglas fir
(*Pseudotsuga menziesii*)
Firs: Balsam and **White** (*Abies balsamea*) (*A. concolor*)

Magnolia, Southern
(*Magnolia grandiflora*)
Oak, Live (*Quercus agrifolia*)
Pines: Eastern white
(*P. strobus*)
Ponderosa
(*Pinus ponderosa*)
Red (*P. resinosa*)
Redwood, Coastal
(*Sequoia sempervirens*)

BELOW HORIZONTAL, DESCENDING ATTACHMENT

Cedar, Deodar
(*Cedrus deodara*)
Pine, Scotch (*Pinus sylvestris*)
Spruces: Brewer's and **Norway**
(*Picea brewerana, P. abies*)

NATURAL EVERGREEN BRANCHING PATTERNS: Many conifers cooperate by naturally growing limbs at a 90° angle. Yet others actually grow down toward the ground (growing against the guidelines of tip-bud dominance). You can try to change these angles, but only with great difficulty or effort. Again, when you buy a new tree, ask about the natural branching pattern.

EVERGREEN TREE SCAFFOLD SHAPES: You should nurture every tree by carefully shaping and pruning the young trunk and main branches that form the core of a healthy, long-lived tree. By pruning with great care in formative years of a tree, it can continue to grow with little or no pruning. Conifers often grow like central leader trees, with a triangular or columnar shape. (Several notable exceptions are the round shapes of the Montezuma, pitch, and Chinese pines.)

CENTRAL LEADER SHAPE: Pruning conifers as central leader trees is basically the same as pruning deciduous trees. However, there are two important distinctions: Do not cut back into bare branches or limbs, because in most cases, nothing will sprout. The exception to this rule, called "random branching," are all arborvitae (*Thuja* spp.), junipers (*Juniperus* spp.), and yews (*taxus* spp.). A simple method used to encourage bushiness (stimulate side shoots) is done by cutting a conifer's "candles" by one-third to one-half during spring growth. When training central leader broadleaf evergreens, follow the same steps that are outlined for central leader deciduous trees (see page 121).

OPEN-CENTER AND DELAYED OPEN-CENTER SHAPES: Most conifers don't naturally grow with an open center—they're unsuited to this form. If you must control the habit, especially the height of a conifer, you can remove the leader after a number of years. This removal should not be done until the tree has matured somewhat. Refrain from pruning into bare growth; instead, cut to existing side shoots or trim the candles. Broadleaf trees may be somewhat more adaptable to delayed open-center pruning; the technique is the same as with deciduous trees (see page 121).

THE STANDARD SHAPE: A standard tree form is most commonly a central leader tree with the lower limbs removed. This style is not found naturally. In fact, it is largely an invention of landscapers and other garden design professionals. While it will not stunt a tree's growth, many gardeners find the shape unnatural looking. This technique is frequently used in public parks to create open spaces beneath the crown. If you like the standard look, use summer pruning to remove unwanted limbs. Like deciduous trees, the limbs are often removed to a level that makes it comfortable to walk beneath. Slightly staggering the height of each limb promotes a less regimented look and is preferred by many gardeners.

Norway spruce

BOTANICAL NAME: *Picea abies*

PLANT TYPE: Evergreen Tree (conifer)

SIZE: Will grow 100'–150' tall, but narrow. Other species of spruces and dwarf varieties don't get as tall and rarely require pruning.

GROWING HABITS: In its youth, an attractive, somewhat narrow, pyramidal shape with a rich, green foliage. As a mature conifer, there are more drooping lower limbs, and some near the ground naturally die back. Well-behaved growth that seldom requires corrective pruning.

TIME TO PRUNE: In its youth, the tree can be sheared for a fuller foliage from midsummer through late summer.

NEW SHOOTS AFTER CUTTING BARE STEMS? Don't cut back to older, bare branches or limbs unless you like bleak stubs.

SPECIAL PRUNING POINTERS: Use routine removal of dead, crossing, storm-damaged, or diseased growth.

STEP BY STEP: *1.* Spring planting from containers or as balled-and-burlapped stock; or late summer or fall planting from containers. If leader is weak, use figure-eight ties to hold the trunk below the leader loosely to a stake. The leader must move in the wind in order to develop strong tissue. Best to plant and leave unpruned until new growth develops. Make sure central leader remains uncut. *2.* Shear candles while young as easy-to-reach crown can be filled in. Make sure no other tip bud tries to outgrow the central leader—head back the competing shoot. *3.* As the tree matures, you can use summer thinning cuts to remove lower limbs before they wither and fall.

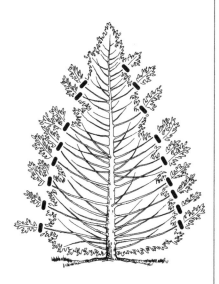

Before: To make a young Norway spruce look full and thick, use heading cuts. For an especially artistic look, use candle pruning techniques. If that is too time-consuming, shearing will do.

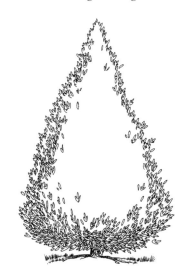

After: A well-shaped spruce makes a good specimen or screen.

American holly

BOTANICAL NAME: *Ilex opaca*

PLANT TYPE: Evergreen Tree (Broadleaf)

SIZE: Most vigorous unnamed species can grow to 50'. Cultivars grow to as short as 6'.

GROWING HABITS: Slow-growing broadleaf, sometimes with showy red (also orange, yellow, and black) berries. Naturally forms a pyramidal, sometimes rounded, crown. Usually grows with a central leader and needs a male and female tree to make red berries. (Some female plants of *I. aquifolium* and hybrids bloom without a nearby male holly.) Makes summer-flowering shoots that form in late summer on the current season's growth.

TIME TO PRUNE: Unpruned trees will probably make the most berries. Because the holly makes summer-flowering shoots, a light shearing in spring will not severely reduce bloom. But don't shear hard in midsummer or developing flower buds will be entirely removed.

NEW SHOOTS AFTER CUTTING BARE STEMS? Yes.

SPECIAL PRUNING POINTERS: Use thoughtful passive resistance for most holly trees (hedges are a different story), and don't prune unless absolutely necessary.

STEP BY STEP: *1.* Prune newly planted hollies only if shoots are damaged or grossly misplaced. Use heading cuts to make more shoots. *2.* If the central leader withers or dies, you can sometimes tie a shoot up as its replacement. Leave the shoot tied to a stake for just one summer and it should stiffen in the vertical position. Remove the stake so the new leader can bend and sway in the wind. *3.* Shear sides of the tree

when it's young if you want to make a thicker canopy. Use a hedge shears and prune only in early to mid spring if you want berries. Using hand shears will cause less damage to the foliage.

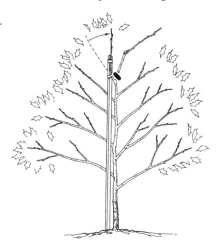

Before: Preserve the pyramidal shape of an American holly with a damaged leader by tying a nearby upright shoot to a stake to replace the leader.

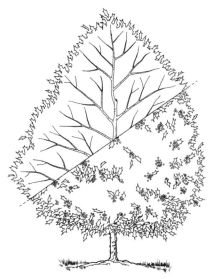

After: Shearing hollies in early to mid spring is optional.

Fruit *and* Nut Trees

F ruit and nut trees are an asset to the home garden. There are very few experiences like reaping a harvest from a backyard orchard nurtured by your own hand. Homegrown fruits and nuts offer the gardener a wide range of variety choices above and beyond what's available at the average supermarket. Also, fruit can be plucked at perfect ripeness, unlike the sundry methods of nonorganic, commercial fruit growers.

Cultivating and pruning fruit and nut trees can be a very rewarding process, but it tends to require more attention than trees and shrubs that do not bear fruit. As you would with any tree, choose carefully when you decide to plant and grow fruit trees. Make sure that you are not only picking a tree that is appropriate for its desired location, but hardy enough for your climate.

Deciduous Fruit and Nut Trees

M any of the fruits and nuts that we covet come from deciduous trees: almonds, apples, apricots, cherries, chestnuts, figs, filberts (hazelnuts), hickory nuts, jujubes, nectarines, peaches, Asian and European pears, pecans, persimmons, European and Japanese plums, pomegranates, quinces, and walnuts.

These fruits will appear nearly every year from the tree without pruning. And, unpruned trees often produce more fruit during their first

This well-shaped apple tree has branches ideally spaced along the trunk, with productive broad branch angles.

10 to 15 years than pruned trees. In fact, the heavier the tree is pruned during this time, the lower the yields.

So why prune? Fruit from unpruned deciduous fruit trees has clear disadvantages. The fruit may be up to one-third smaller than fruit from a pruned tree. Fruit that is shaded by the canopy will not have fully colored skin. And, all the fruit is formed farther from the center of the tree each year on newer spurs or terminal shoots. Some spurs can be productive for years or even decades, but it's the shade of an unpruned canopy that starves older spurs nearer to the center of the tree. The lack of sunlight causes the spurs to wither, die, and become similar to trace buds on older bark. Thus, the new fruit develops farther from reach with each passing year and a ladder becomes essential for harvesting. Heavy bearing on the ends of branches often causes them to break off, inviting infection and rot.

Pruning deciduous fruit and nut trees allows ample sunshine in the lower portion of the crown and encourages fruiting spurs to produce good-sized, highly colored fruit. Regular pruning will also keep growth compact enough to make cutting and harvesting conveniently within easy reach.

PRUNING FOR SIZE AND LIGHT: When pruning fruit trees it is important to maintain a tree size that is manageable and healthy. A crown that is pruned to allow light into its center will foster evenly sized, well-colored fruit or nuts. Abide by these two general guidelines and your trees will repay you with fruit and longevity.

The various sizes and shapes of fruit trees determine the crown's light levels. Older, full-sized crowns—on open-center trees or delayed open-center trees—look the most imposing, and their shape often shades up to 30% of the lower canopy, which is too dark to sustain healthy fruiting spurs. To control this habit, central leader trees are dependent on dwarfing rootstock to maintain a smaller size. A heavily dwarfing rootstock will encourage a crown size conducive to getting enough light to sustain the spurs. Dwarf fruit trees are also much more productive per square foot of your yard than standard-size fruit trees.

Each of the basic fruit tree shapes has a unique set of pruning criterion. Space considerations and personal preferences should be taken into account when determining which shape is best for your tree. It's also important to consider the long-term health of your fruit trees as certain shapes will weaken trees as they mature.

OPEN-CENTER TREES: The traditional shape for full-size, open-center fruit trees are shaped like a wide-mouthed vase or goblet. When dormant-planted, these trees are traditionally cut back to a stick 3' tall. The lower limbs—which form after the spring pruning—are attached to the trunk 2' to 3' above the ground. This shape was originally developed so tractors could easily pass beneath the widening limbs. When using a mower or permanent mulch below the tree, you can cut the maiden (young trunk) lower so fruit forms close to the ground in easy reach. Paint the trunk with white latex paint to protect the young bark from sunburn.

After the spring pruning, do not let the first shoot below the cut sprout vertically to become another leader or trunk. Shape this vertical shoot to a 45°–60° angle using some type of spreader. Make sure all the side shoots are growing

TRUNK PAINTING

Fruit trees are planted so close together at wholesale growing grounds that the unnatural amount of shade leaves the bark tender. To safeguard against weakness, paint the trunk of a new tree up into the lower branches with a 50/50 solution of water and white interior or exterior latex paint. This one-time application of paint will reflect light from the trunk and keep the bark's temperature down. By the time the paint flakes off and the new bark shows through, it will be tough enough to endure any amount of direct sunlight.

at a wide angle of attachment to maintain the shape. By midsummer, select which shoots are to be permanent limbs that will form the primary scaffold. These limbs should be spread as far apart as possible along the trunk and equally around its circumference. Remove any crowding or unwanted shoots with a quick snip of the shears.

The following spring after planting, head all previous year's growth back to stimulate more side branching, making good use of air space. Advice varies on how far to head back new growth; you can cut back by one-third or one-half on one-year-old shoots. Both lengths can work, but you'll have to judge which is best for your particular tree. The main goal is to fill the space above the trunk with side branches for more fruit. Vigorous branches need less pruning to encourage side shoots, but weaker growth needs heavier pruning to induce new shoots. In all cases, make sure the first bud below the heading cut is on the underside of the shoot facing outward.

Use weights, toothpicks, clothespins, or twine to make sure all new growth is at the ideal angle—45°–60°—for growth and flower formation. In the summer, watch for wayward shoots, vertical watersprouts, or root suckers, and remove them with thinning cuts. Be sure to remove root suckers below the ground where they're attached to the roots.

Each year after the shape has been established, use summer pruning to remove any limbs or shoots that are casting too much shade. Conversely, make sure the foliage in the center of the tree isn't too thin, as sunscald will damage top branches of the primary scaffold, especially in hot-summer climates. Sunburned branches or limbs often fail to form calluses, making a permanent place for the entry of debilitating diseases, fungi, and rots.

In old age, the open-center tree is the weakest of all fruit tree shapes. As the tree matures, the weight of the limbs and the crop is farther from the trunk each year. The weight can leverage limbs off the trunk and sometimes all of the

For delayed open-center training, remove the leader and replace it with the closest side branch in early summer. Repeat each year for up to 5 years.

main limbs split apart at the same time, leaving you with little more than a harvest of firewood.

Where the primary scaffold meets the trunk a pocket can form that collects rain and dirt. Frequently, this union is an area of weakness; a fissure in the trunk, insect damage, or disease can allow water and fungi into the trunk's core and cause the heartwood to rot. The heartwood acts like ballast for the tree and the primary scaffold, adding stability. If rot destroys much of the heartwood, you'll have a hollow tree that can easily fall or be blown over.

DELAYED OPEN-CENTER TREES: This is the sturdiest form for large, long-lived fruit trees. Begin training like an open-center tree—plant a maiden and cut it back to 3' or lower. (Don't forget the white latex paint.) During the first summer, however, make sure the first shoot below the cut trunk or leader grows vertically to replace the removed leader. If the shoot isn't cooperating by early summer, tie a 12" stick to the top of the leader, extending 6" or more above the maiden's top. Using green garden tape, gently tie the recalcitrant shoot to the stick for the summer. By fall, you can remove the ties and stick, and the shoot will remain vertical. Leave all side shoots untouched for the summer so their foliage will build girth and roots. But be sure to shape them to the ideal 45°–60° angle with all the weight or tying tricks at your disposal.

In the second spring, cut the leader back again to cause more side shoots, some of which will become part of the primary scaffold. Make sure the first bud grows to be a replacement for the leader. Cut back any of the first year's laterals that need encouragement to form side branching. Again, leave all new side shoots to build the tree's size and health. Always cut any lateral shoots back to an underneath bud facing out.

Repeat the cutting and regrowth of the leader for five years. Once you have plenty of laterals from which to select the primary scaffold branches, you can permanently remove the leader in summer. The height of the last lateral may be 4"–10" off the ground depending on how many laterals you want and the particular habit of the tree. Also, thin out any crowded laterals so the remaining laterals of the primary scaffold are well spaced on the height and circumference of the trunk. Once the leader has been permanently removed, be certain to cut back any laterals to outside, underneath buds to promote width over height.

CENTRAL LEADER AND MODIFIED LEADER TREES: Many of the pruning tips given for deciduous excurrent ornamental trees (see page 123) with well-defined central leaders apply to this shape for fruit trees. Since the shape is the same, the pruning techniques are similar.

The smaller semidwarf and true dwarf rootstocks are best for central leader trees. Because the roots control the tree to less than 12' tall, you can easily maintain a leader for the life of the tree. With the true semidwarf and larger dwarf trees, you can head back the leader once each spring to guarantee laterals to choose from—thus the official name of "delayed" or "modified" central leader tree. Heading the leader is identical for a delayed open-center tree, but the leader remains for the life of the tree. If the top gets beyond the reach of your stepladder, simply remove the leader during the summer.

Strongly dwarfing rootstocks keep the crown under 8' and make a true central leader tree. With these short trees, the leader is never cut unless the tree fails to produce adequate laterals.

DECIDUOUS TERMINAL-FRUITING NUT AND FRUIT TREES

Chestnuts (*Castanea* ssp.)
Figs (*Ficus* ssp.)
Filbert (hazelnuts)
  (*Corylus maxima*)
Hickory nuts (*Carya* ssp.)
Pecans (*C. Illinoinensis*)
Persimmon
  (*Diospyros virginiana, D. kaki*)
  (American and Japanese)
Pomegranate
  (*Punica granatum*)
Quince
  (*Cydonia oblonga*)
Walnut (*Juglans* ssp.)

SPUR-TYPE FRUIT TREES: Spur-type trees can be trained into any of the previously discussed shapes. Your pruning focus will be on the first year's growth each season. By shaping and pruning the new shoots, you can encourage more flower buds and greater fruiting for many years. Again, positioning the new shoot to a 45°–60° angle is often all that's required for healthy flower-bud formation.

If you still don't get as many flower buds as you want, or there are none in places where you want them, notching is your next best option. Use a ⅜" round rat-tail file to score halfway around the stem and below each dormant bud.

If all goes well, you will have abundant spur growth with plenty of branching in the spur system. If there are good sets of blossoms and plenty of fruit, a fruitful spur system may become so laden with fruit that pieces of it are snapped.

TERMINAL-FRUITING NUT AND FRUIT TREES: Deciduous nut and fruit trees that form fruit on the new growth *after* spring growth has begun are called terminal bearers. Most nut trees come under this category (the notable exception is the almond tree).

Because these trees bear their crop on the ends of new growth, pruning is simplified. These trees may continue to bear without pruning more predictably than spur-type fruit trees. Pruning can be done with less attention to detail since some uncut tips will surely be left and these will bear a marginally smaller crop.

Begin by removing all dead, damaged, diseased, and crossing growth. As you would for all fruiting trees, prune for the overall shape you desire—open-center, delayed open-center, central leader (except for nut trees), or espalier (except for nut trees). Shape the tree to be as low as possible for an easy harvest (not needed with chestnuts, hickory nuts, and pecans because the crop falls to the ground).

Whenever possible, use thinning cuts to prune back a well-placed shoot, branch, or limb. At the same time, prune for branches that will be strong enough to support the crop. This is done by using heading cuts to reduce the length of existing branches and limbs to properly placed laterals or branches.

Because terminal-fruiting trees are so easy to prune, all but the nut trees make good medium- to full-sized espalier fruit trees with both informal and formal shapes (see page 152).

Asian pear, European pear

BOTANICAL NAMES: *Pyrus ussuriensis, P. cummunis*

PLANT TYPE: Deciduous Fruit Tree

SIZE: Trees on standard rootstocks can reach 45' tall by 25' wide. (Asian pear trees on *Pyrus betulifolia* rootstock can grow 40' tall.) A number of dwarfing rootstocks are available that can reduce the size to 11'–16' tall and 8'–12' wide.

GROWING HABITS: Vigorous growth. Spur-type fruiting. Spurs stay fruitful for more than five years. European pears are inclined to make a good number of side branches without

Asian pear, European pear *(continued)*

pruning. Asian pears, however, are less likely to produce side shoots without spring heading. Both types have a strong tendency to produce narrow angles of attachment—Asian pears even more so than European trees. Both make a fairly large number of flower buds without much shaping. They also bear at the tips of some growth. The weight of fruit will lower the tips of branches, but may also snap the branch off the tree. Proper shaping of all primary scaffold limbs and all branches is important to hold a large crop. (Some thinning of young fruits may still be required.)

TIME TO PRUNE: When planted, these trees need to be cut back firmly to initiate enough side shoots to form into the primary scaffold. These are excellent candidates for delayed open-center pruning. Be sure the first bud on the leader regrows as a new leader for several years. Each spring, cut back any

long, unbranched growth to stimulate side shoots. Pay particular attention to early-summer shaping of the main branches for wide angles of attachment that will slow down the tip bud and make a few more side shoots.

NEW SHOOTS AFTER CUTTING BARE STEMS? Cutting back anywhere will surely produce new growth. Old trees can even get the "chainsaw treatment" to rejuvenate a poor-growing tree. Be sure to strip off all but one of the many shoots that will form after severe pruning. (You may want to leave two or three shoots until late summer and select the best-looking shoot to be the new leader.)

SPECIAL PRUNING POINTERS: The critical part of growing pear trees is to correct their tendency to make narrow, vase-like vertical growth. If shoots grow too long, they can be headed back in the summer to slow them down and encourage side shoots. Always keep an

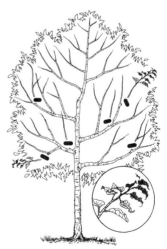

Before: Head back newly planted pear trees to develop new side branches. When suitable lateral branches reach 6"–12" long, spread them with clothespins.

After: Thin back upright growth and remove any fire blight diseased stems to at least 1' below the damage or at the branch collar, sterilizing pruning shears after each cut.

Asian pear, European pear *(continued)*

eye out for fire blight. Cut all visibly damaged growth and at least 12", preferably 18", past the visible damage into clean, green growth. Be sure to cleanse your pruning shear's blades *after each cut* with a 10% bleach-and-water solution, 100% Lysol,™ or 100% rubbing alcohol.

STEP BY STEP: *1.* To fashion a central leader tree, buy a maiden bare-root tree with a dwarfing rootstock. (If you can find a tree with well-placed branches, you can skip cutting back the tree.) *2.* Clip the leader to about 6"–12" above the graft on the maiden. (Each year the leader can be cut back in the spring in order to encourage a new set of lateral shoots. Make sure the first shoot below the cut regrows as the delayed or modified central leader.) *3.* Also at planting, head back any branches by one-third to one-half to provoke more side shoots. *4.* Be sure to use toothpicks or clothespins to spread any narrow shoots in early summer. *5.* Pear trees often make plenty of vertical growth; remove as needed with summer thinning cuts. *6.* Young pear shoots not destined to become permanent branches or the primary scaffold are particularly suited to arching with weights—one or more clothespins are easy to use and effective. This will make fruit on the outer third of the arched growth. The weight of the first year's crop will carry on the arching effect and the clothespins should be removed.

Japanese plum

BOTANICAL NAME: *Prunus salicina*

PLANT TYPE: Deciduous Fruit Tree

SIZE: On standard plum rootstocks, up to 18'–20' tall by 16'–18' wide. The only decent dwarfing rootstock, Citation™, reduces the size by only 10% to 20%.

GROWING HABITS: Spur-type fruiting tree. The spurs stay fruitful for up to five years. Even more vaselike and vertical than pear trees. Fast, vigorous growth can easily get out of control with tall watersprouts and less fruitful vertical growth. Prone to make double leaders on both the trunk and the branches. Always cut off one of the double shoots. Will bear well without pruning, but fruits are small, hard to reach, and branches may break off from the weight of the fruit.

TIME TO PRUNE: Many bare-root plum trees come with a number of branches. If this is the case, head back the leader 6"–12" above the last major branch to form the next set of laterals. While plum shoots are not as easily trained to a wide angle as pear shoots, every effort should be made to shape *all* new shoots to a wider angle. Summer shaping and pruning are essential to counteract the vaselike shape. Where the plums ripen by midsummer and the cold of fall does not arrive early, exclusive summer pruning has been used successfully to control growth and favor fruit production. This timing avoids forcing too much unwanted growth with typical spring pruning.

NEW SHOOTS AFTER CUTTING BARE STEMS? This tree will sprout new shoots easily. Cut to any bare growth and an abundance of shoots will arise.

Japanese plum *(continued)*

SPECIAL PRUNING POINTERS: Pruning in the summer can help avoid cytospora canker disease (also called perennial canker), bacterial gummosis (*Pseudomonas syringae*), and bacterial canker (*P. mors-prunorum*). These diseases spread easily into pruning wounds during wet, mild spring weather. This tree makes root suckers easily, especially if the roots are damaged by cultivation or tillage. Remove suckers once the shoots have stiffened.

STEP BY STEP: *1.* Most plum trees are trained as open-center trees. Buy a well-branched bare-root tree with well-placed branches for an open-center form. *2.* Clip the new tree's leader to about 6"–12" above the graft on a maiden. Remove any shoots that try to regrow as the leader, or shape them to a wide angle as a new branch. The leader can be removed in the spring to encourage a new set of lateral shoots. *3.* With a well-branched tree, head back any branches by one-third to one-half to provoke more side shoots in the spring. Also, make sure that the middle of the tree has enough foliage to prevent sunburn to the primary scaffold. *4.* Be sure to use toothpicks or clothespins to spread any narrow shoots in early summer. Do not go easy on the summer shaping; this is critical to a well-shaped and fruitful tree. Because the plum tree is less likely to have enough laterals for prolific fruiting, spreading older growth will have to be done with sticks with nail points. *5.* Plum trees make even more vertical growth than pear trees. With your thumb, rub out any unwanted vertical shoots, or use summer thinning cuts. *6.* Remove suckers by midsummer or as soon as is convenient.

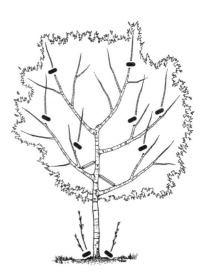

Before: Train into an open-center shape by removing the leader in spring. Thin back unproductive, upright growth and remove suckers. Use spreaders for shaping limbs into correct position.

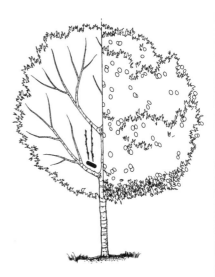

After: Continue to remove any vertical suckers or sprouts. Each spring, when dormant, head back branches by ⅓ to encourage new side shoots to develop.

EVERGREEN FRUIT AND NUT TREES

Evergreen fruit and nut trees share one common trait: they don't make spur-type growth, but bear their crops on terminal and co-terminal growth. Most evergreen fruit and nut trees are subtropical or tropical plants that are easy to grow in the proper climate. If left unpruned, they bear abundantly; when pruned heavily, they'll often make a suitable crop. Evergreen fruit offers many benefits to the home garden: "edible hedges," many attractive types of foliage, and, in some areas, trees and shrubs that are nearly free of pests and diseases. Unfortunately, their general intolerance of freezing temperatures limits their suitability to the southeastern, southern, southwestern, and central Californian coastlines, or permanent confinement to greenhouse cultivation.

These scrumptious trees come in many forms; the multi-trunked pineapple guava (*Feijoa sellowiana*) can be shaped as a hedge or trained as a

TERMINAL-BEARING FRUIT AND NUT TREES

There are many options for these luscious additions to any garden or edible landscape. Here's a short list of some options.

Avocado (*Persea americana*) (Mexican varieties may tolerate 24°F.)

Cherimoya (*Annona cherimola*) (Tolerates light frost.)

Citrus (*Citrus* spp.) (High variable; foliage damaged at 26°–28°F, 'Kumquats' hardy to 18°F, 'Mexican limes' damaged at 32°F, Lemons at about 28°F.)

Guava, Strawberry/Lemon (*Psidium cattleianum*) (Tolerates some frost.)

Loquat (*Eriobotrya japonica*) (Hardy to 20°F.)

Macadamia nuts (*Macadamia* spp.) (Hardy to about 25°F.)

Mango (*Mangifera indica*) (Hardy to 30°F.)

Olive (*Olea europaea*) (Leaves damaged at 12°F, green fruit damaged at 28°F.)

Papaya, Mountain (*Carica pubescens*) (Damage below 28°F.)

Pineapple guava (not a true guava) (*Feijoa sellowiana*) (Hardy to 15°F.)

Plum, Natal (*Carissa macrocarpa*) (Tolerates into upper 20°s F.)

Sapote, White (*Casimiroa edulis*) (About as hardy as true lemon.)

single-trunked 15'-to-25'-tall standard tree; the 25'-to-40'-tall by 40'-wide, dark green crown of an avocado grows as a frumpy version of an umbrella—mostly as a single trunk and occasionally with multiple trunks.

PRUNING FOR LIGHT: Good-tasting, quality fruit is dependent on light reaching the fruit to add a rich color and an appetizing, complex taste. But more than any other type of tree, evergreen fruit and nut trees are sensitive to sunburn. Once portions of the trunk or limbs are damaged by too much sun, the damaged tissue rarely calluses and the permanently exposed wound is an entry point for rot and insects. All of these plants should have their trunk and a portion of their limbs painted with a 50/50 mix of white interior or exterior *latex* paint and water the day they're planted.

It's important to prune these trees and shrubs with caution—especially in the summer. Achieving the right balance is important; removing too much foliage will cause the dreaded sunburn, and too little pruning will produce a less desirable crop in the interior of the crown. It's better to err on the side of too little pruning as sunburn often becomes a permanent liability. Only time and experience will give each gardener, in each unique microclimate, the wisdom to know the proper amount of thinning for each crown.

PRUNING FOR SHAPE: Because of their terminal-bearing habit, these trees and shrubs are very adaptable to both neglect and severe pruning. On full-sized trees or shrubs, make sure they have sturdy central leaders that will support the primary scaffold and the fruit or nut crop. Remove with thinning cuts any shoots that threaten to outgrow the central leader. The goal of pruning all terminal-bearing trees is to achieve the right shape (primarily done in summer) because they fruit abundantly, regardless of branch position. Allow the crown to grow to a natural form, only stepping in to prune out long, lanky growth or branches that are not able to carry an abundant crop.

The basics of pruning still apply, with a few special considerations. Always remove dead, damaged, diseased, and crossing stems, branches, or limbs as soon as you notice the problem. Be careful to time your pruning; spring pruning risks damage to subsequent new growth from late frosts; late summer or fall pruning can lead to damage from early freezes. Reduce the length of branches with heading cuts to properly placed laterals or branches. Remove unwanted branches with thinning cuts to the branch collar. Watch for too little shade to protect the primary scaffold. If there is enough shade from the canopy, there's no need to paint young trunks or exposed limbs. Shape the tree to be as low as possible for an easy harvest by always cutting to the outward-facing buds on the underside of the shoot.

EDIBLE HEDGES: Many terminal-bearing plants make great hedges. They are easily confined to just about any shape and will still make some fruit. Examples of edible hedges include citrus, lemon guava, natal plum, olive, pineapple guava, and strawberry guava. Prune these plants as you would an evergreen hedge.

It's much easier to form a hedge if you can purchase plants with multiple trunks. If you can only find plants with a single trunk, cut the leader back to near the ground the first spring to stimulate multiple shoots. In the summer, thin out any weakly attached or crowded shoots by rubbing them off with your fingers. If growth is adequate, you may be able to shear back the new multiple shoots in early summer to awaken more lateral growth.

It is critical with these cold-intolerant plants that you don't prune too late in the summer or too early in spring and expose succulent new growth to possible frosts. If you live in a marginal climate for these plants, be sure to tarp the young plants during cold nights. Use stakes to form a shelter so that the sheet or tarp doesn't touch the foliage. As the plants mature, they will become slightly hardier.

Pineapple guava

BOTANICAL NAME: *Feijoa sellowiana*

PLANT TYPE: Evergreen Fruit Tree

SIZE: Height and width is 18'–25' when unpruned.

GROWING HABITS: Often a multi-trunk small tree or shrub with a lovely orange-brown textured bark. Slow-growing unless well fertilized and watered regularly. Gorgeous flowers with dramatic tufts of red stamens surrounded by pinkish white, fleshy petals—which are flavored and make great additions to fruit salads and ice cream. The flowers are terminal and occur in late spring or early summer on current year's growth.

Pineapple guava *(continued)*

The 3"–4" dull green fruit have insignificant seeds and a richly aromatic tropical pineapple-like taste. Growth is well branched without pruning. Leaves are an attractive glossy green on top and silver-gray beneath.

TIME TO PRUNE: In frost-free areas, you can prune just about anytime. In all other climates, especially near the edge of the plant's range, late-spring pruning will escape late frosts but still cause laterals to form. Summer pruning can be used to control unwanted growth with thinning cuts.

NEW SHOOTS AFTER CUTTING BARE STEMS? Will sprout new shoots.

SPECIAL PRUNING POINTERS: No spreaders, twine, or weights required

for stimulating fruit as the terminal-bearing occurs naturally. Be aware of the fruit still ripening on the tree when doing summer pruning. Can be sheared heavily to form a standard, a topiary, or a hedge.

STEP BY STEP: *1.* Purchase a multi-trunk specimen for a more attractive trunk line. If the only available plants have single trunks, cut back in late spring to stimulate new shoots (due to removal of the tip buds) to convert into a multi-trunk. *2.* Shear back as required in the summer until sometime in August, depending on how early your first frost arrives. Heavy shearing will eliminate much of the crop, but any new shoots in the following spring will bear if left unclipped.

Citrus

BOTANICAL NAME: *Citrus* spp.

SIZE: Varies considerably from variety to variety. Up to 25' tall and wide with oranges, 15'–20' for 'Bears' lime trees. Good dwarfing rootstocks (trifoliate orange or 'Hiryu' ['Flying Dragon']) can keep any citrus, with pruning, to less than 5' with some effort.

GROWING HABITS: While terminal-bearing, the different varieties bear fruit on the outside of the foliage or, to varying degrees, beneath the foliage. For a citrus hedge, choose a variety that bears within the foliage. Examples include 'Washington Navel' and 'Valencia' oranges (*not* 'Robertson Navel' oranges), 'Tarocco' blood oranges (*not* 'Sanguinelli' or 'Moro' blood oranges), and 'Lisbon' and 'Improved Meyer' lemons. Citrus trees are well branched without prun-

ing. Sometimes they make trunk and rootstock suckers. Dwarfing rootstocks are prone to suckering, and the resulting sucker growth does not resemble the variety's foliage.

TIME TO PRUNE: As a full-sized tree needs little pruning. Mature trees need only removal of dead, damaged, diseased, and crossing branches or limbs, usually with thinning cuts. All pruning should be done well after the last spring frost and before fall's first freeze. Cut watersprouts to the branch collar or head back and prune to make it fruitful by controlling its growth to the overall shape of the tree. Rootstock suckers must be removed to the point of their origin during midsummer.

NEW SHOOTS AFTER CUTTING BARE STEMS? Will sprout from old branches, limbs, or on the trunk.

Citrus *(continued)*

SPECIAL PRUNING POINTERS: Be aware that some citrus have thorny shoots—especially on new growth and from trunk or rootstock sucker growth. Puncture wounds from the thorns are easily infected and can cause serious illness. If you have the slightest concern about too much light hitting exposed branches, limbs, or the trunk, paint the bark with white latex paint (interior or exterior, diluted by 50% with water).

STEP BY STEP: *1.* Buy only a well-shaped plant with a sturdy central leader. When possible, avoid trees tied to a stake in their container because the trunk will have a smaller diameter. Prune off wayward growth or broken shoots of branches after planting. *2.* As the tree grows, thin out or head back any shoot that outgrows the shape you desire for the canopy. *3.* To form a hedge, simply shear it in the late spring and in the early or late summer as needed. The crop may be reduced, but in the proper climate there will still be plenty of fruit to harvest. If possible, avoid pruning when in full bloom. However, some citrus bloom virtually year-round in the ideal climate—so you may have to reduce the harvest in order to shape a hedge.

ESPALIER

Espalier trees conjure up a range of emotions in gardeners, depending on their experience. Those who have seen wondrous examples of espalier trees, especially fruiting versions, feel inspired and enraptured. Gardeners who have leapt into the culture of an espalier tree or shrub and were left with mangled, misshapen remains of

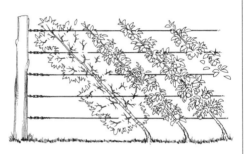

a plant will feel chagrined. And the few who have mastered the most challenging horticultural work of art rightfully feel proud, if not exceptional—and justifiably so. One of the differences that separates the dissatisfied gardener from the pleased one is the style, form, and success of their espaliers.

ESPALIER TREES AND SHRUBS

The first choice in choosing an espalier is one of style—informal and formal. Informal espalier trees or shrubs are mostly trained flat against a wall, a trellis, or a set of wires. These are almost two-dimensional plants—lots of width and perhaps height, but little depth. They have a random collection of branches and limbs that are disguised—at least during the spring and summer—by the plant's foliage. They often resemble a clinging vine.

Formal espaliers are the architectural wonders so frequently displayed in dreamy photographs that appear in elegant, ostentatious books and magazines. The notable feature of a formal espalier is the meticulously defined line of the branches and limbs. These often take the form of flat candelabras or T- and U-shaped trees, all laden with fruit. Some of the principal forms of these precisely arranged plants are vertical cordon, double and single horizontal cordons, palmette oblique, palmette ver-rier, Belgian fence, U-shaped, horizontal-T, oblique cordon, and Belgian arch (arcure method). These forms are representative of the high art of the espalier.

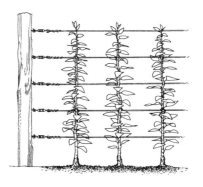

Vertical cordon: Great against walls

The pruner's next option is to choose between ornamental and fruiting espalier trees and shrubs. Ornamental espaliers are grown solely for their foliage. Those that feature only the color and texture of the foliage, no matter what style, are far less difficult than any blooming, ornamental espalier. The foliage-based espalier requires frequent shearing to remove unwanted growth and removal of tip buds to stimulate more lateral shoots. Don't concern your-self with pruning for bloom or structure and pattern of the branches and limbs—except with deciduous varieties.

Another espalier choice involves mixing foliage color and texture with the color of the bloom, which adds another dimension to this style. Any attractive flowering tree or shrub can be trained to an informal style, although some will be much larger than others. Some ornamental trees and shrubs lend themselves better to the espalier form, most notably the terminal- and co-terminal-flowering plants. If the pruning is not too severe, these will easily bloom from new, uncut growth each spring.

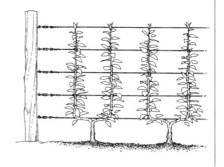

Double cordon: Easy and sophisticated

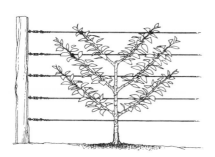

*Palmette oblique: Makes use of 45°
branch angles*

Finally, there are the fruiting espaliers—especially deciduous fruiting trees—which are one of horticulture's loftiest goals, a botanical Mount Everest if you will. These forms combine the architecture of an espalier with the taste of luscious ripe fruit—a magical combination that is not easy to attain. The difficulties with fruiting espaliers arise from many conflicting aspects; most forms of espalier are not naturally suitable for making fruit (remember, tip buds

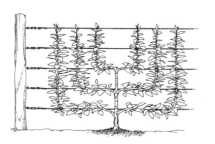

Palmette verrier: Elegant on a trellis

want to grow vertically and not make fruit) so vigilant effort is required to encourage certain plants to produce adequate yields of fruit. The reason for this is dormant buds on growth quickly bent to a horizontal angle naturally want to make vertical, unfruitful shoots. Thus the palmette oblique, all vertical and horizontal cordons, palmette verrier, and horizontal-T forms are biologically inclined to make vegetative growth, not flower and fruit. With these styles, the gardener must spend many hours shaping, bending, tying, clipping, and generally coercing flower and fruit from a plant whose very genetic impulses are opposed to fruiting in such forms.

Instead, those gardeners inspired to cultivate fruiting espalier trees should consider forms that naturally lend themselves to a healthy balance of vegetative and flowering growth. The Belgian fence and oblique cordon both take advantage of the ideal 45° angle, which pro-

U-shaped: May yield large fruit

motes some new shoot growth and a healthy amount of flower buds. Also, the Belgian arch makes plenty of fruit on the outside of each arched branch, as would any weeping deciduous fruit tree branch. These three styles are the best for beginning espalier enthusiasts because the flow of hormones and food together work in favor of producing fruit and flowers.

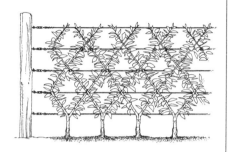

Belgian fence: A pretty screen

No matter what the style or form, be sure to have a firm, sturdy structure to support any espalier. The possibilities are numerous and depend on a range of factors. Take into consideration the type tree or shrub that you are trying to espalier. Different plants will have growing habits more suited to a very sturdy structure, like a brick wall. There is almost nothing more frustrating than spending months training a prized plant into an espalier form only to have it ruined by a failed support system.

Growing espalier trees on a freestanding trellis made of wooden or metal posts firmly cemented into the ground, with high-tensile wire strung in rows is a common method. While it's not foolproof, it's quite effective and relatively hassle free. The turnbuckles keep the wire taut. The same high-tensile wire with turnbuckles can be strung between eyebolts set 6"–12" away from a cement wall, a cinder-block wall, or a wooden fence. Also, wooden, metal rebar, or bar metal lattice supports, can be bracketed 6"–12" away from a wall. With enough money, you can construct a freestanding fancy wrought-iron or bent metal-pipe framework to match the espalier pattern you desire.

T-shaped: A low fence for around the garden

Crape myrtle

BOTANICAL NAME: *Lagerstroemia indica*

PLANT TYPE: Deciduous Ornamental Informal Espalier Tree

SIZE: Unpruned tree to 208' tall and 12'–15' wide. Espalier to 8'–15' tall and almost as wide. Cultivars can be anywhere from 3'–10' tall whether they are espaliered or not.

GROWING HABITS: Slow-growing with an attractive bark and sculptural branches. Showy flowers form on current season's growth in late summer on summer-flowering shoots.

TIME TO PRUNE: Prune heavily in late winter or early spring to control form and stimulate new shoots for flower. Prune after flowering to control unwanted or excessive growth. Deadhead flowers after they've bloomed.

NEW SHOOTS AFTER CUTTING BARE STEMS? Yes.

SPECIAL PRUNING POINTERS: Can get heavy mildew in some climates—train to an open-wire trellis (not against a wall or fence) to allow plenty of air circulation. Look for resistant varieties; they are named for Indian tribes— 'Cherokee', 'Natchez', and 'Muskogee' are examples.

STEP BY STEP: (Best done as an espalier in warmer winter climates.) *1.* Choose a plant with multiple trunks or a well-branched specimen. Plant next to a sturdy trellis system and train in an open, informal fan shape to allow good air circulation. *2.* Fill in the width by allowing some side branches to grow with their tip bud uncut. Allow the tip bud to grow vertically to a suitable length. During the summer—once the shoot is long enough—tie the vertical portion of the shoot down to fill in the form. The tip may stop growing if the shoot is lowered to a horizontal position, but you've already given it the length the espalier's shape needs. *3.* In early spring, head back some branches to make lateral growth. Leave enough tip buds intact on some of the fan branches to encourage extension of the fan shape. Head back some shoots or laterals to make more spring growth

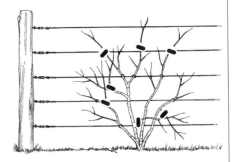

Before: Train a multiple-trunked tree into a flat plane with branches evenly spaced on the trellis. Head back some upright growth to encourage further branching. Tie desired branches to the trellis.

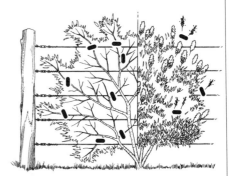

After: To maintain the informal espalier, use thinning and heading cuts to shape and control size. Remove old flowers.

Crape myrtle *(continued)*

to form the late summer's blooms. Do not shear; make each cut selectively with a hand clipper. Remember, the deciduous branching pattern will show all winter, so some attention to detail with the fan-shaped primary scaffold will be worth the effort. *4.* In summer, tie the primary branches to the trellis as they grow. Tie them at least 8" back from the tip bud to prevent slowing the new growth. Thin out unwanted growth. Head back new shoots to fill in any blank areas. Over time, retrain replacement branches for the primary fan shape. Remove any twiggy growth.

Southern or Evergreen magnolia

BOTANICAL NAME: *Magnolia grandiflora*

PLANT TYPE: Evergreen Ornamental Informal Espalier Tree

SIZE: Unpruned, 60'–100' tall and 30'–50' feet wide, often less. The cultivar 'Little Gem' is under 20' tall and wide. There are other shorter cultivars.

GROWING HABITS: Glorious glossy dark green leaves with velvetlike reddish brown underside. Slow to grow if left unfertilized and unwatered. Can improve growth with regular care. Fantastic creamy-white flowers in early or midsummer on current season's growth—terminal-flowering shoots. Usually pest-free.

TIME TO PRUNE: Needs little pruning as a garden tree. As a large, informal espalier it needs frequent heading and thinning cuts to keep the foliage from being too dense. Prune in early spring to stimulate shoots.

NEW SHOOTS AFTER CUTTING BARE STEMS? No, not worth the risk of letting rot and disease into the heart of the tree.

SPECIAL PRUNING POINTERS: In the spring, don't cut all shoots or you will eliminate the summer flowering. Ambitious summer pruning after bloom is required to keep the flattened espalier shape.

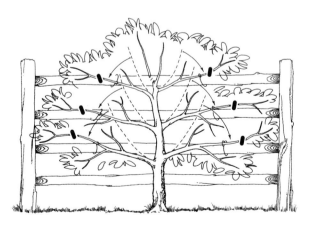

Before: Establish a sturdy trellis for this large tree. Head back some laterals to encourage branching, and thin to shape. Pull branches down and secure to trellis to create a graceful, wide branching angle.

Southern or Evergreen magnolia *(continued)*

STEP BY STEP: *1.* Purchase a well-branched specimen that is young enough to still have pliable branches. Plant next to a wall or structure large enough to accommodate the size of magnolia you purchased. Use sturdy pipe, wood, or metal rebar to fashion a rugged trellis. Use strong ties to fasten the branches to the trellis. Head back some branches to existing laterals in the early spring to help fill in the trellis. Leave some branches uncut so the tip bud will continue to grow. *2.* To fill in the width, allow some side branches to remain uncut. Let the tip bud begin to grow vertically to make length. In the second half of summer, tie the vertical shoots down to the angle you want to fill in the form. *3.* During each summer, prune any rampant growth with hand clippers—use thinning cuts to the branch collar. (Hedge shears will make leaves look ratty.) Since the branching structure won't show beneath the foliage, you can continue to randomly tie to the trellis as many shoots as are required to fill the area. Be sure to *gradually* bend shoots to horizontal. *4.* Don't forget to sit beneath the blooming espalier and soak up the rich, sensuous fragrance.

After: Thin back misplaced or long shoots, using care not to damage the foliage.

Flowering quince

BOTANICAL NAME: *Chaenomeles speciosa*

PLANT TYPE: Deciduous Ornamental Informal Espalier Shrub

SIZE: Grows to 5'–7' tall and wide. Cultivars available that grow 1'–2' tall and wide.

GROWING HABITS: Moderate-growing shrub, often with thorns. Flowers in early spring on last year's growth on second-year-flowering shoots.

TIME TO PRUNE: Severe pruning in the spring will destroy many of the blooms. Best to do majority of pruning after flowering is over.

NEW SHOOTS AFTER CUTTING BARE STEMS? In the garden it's usually pruned by selectively removing old growth with thinning cuts.

SPECIAL PRUNING POINTERS: Watch out for the thorny varieties—wear gloves and a long-sleeved shirt.

STEP BY STEP: *1.* These well-behaved plants don't need as sturdy a trellis as most espaliers need. Plant in early

Flowering quince *(continued)*

spring through midsummer and tie the best branches to the trellis. Remember, this plant is deciduous so branch structure will show all winter. Try using an informal fan shape or curving main branches like a weeping fan.
2. Allow some side shoots to remain uncut so the tip bud will grow vertically and encourage length. Tie the vertical portion of the shoot down progressively over the summer to the angle you need for the desired form. First tie the shoot down by 20°–30° for up to a month, then down another 20°–30° for a month or so, and finally to the position you desire. Thus, you'll use

the plant's flow of hormones to make more flower buds instead of just tying the shoot *directly* to a horizontal position from the onset. 3. In summer, thin any unwanted, rampant growth. Shear heavily up through midsummer to keep the foliage as flat as you want. Because the leaves are not too big, you may be able to use a hedge shears.
4. This plant is prone to making many shoots from the rootstock. Dig down to the sucker's attachment to the root and clip at the equivalent of the branch collar. 5. Leave the plant unpruned in the spring to encourage bloom.

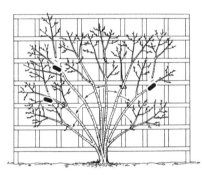

Before: In spring, tie down the main branches to a trellis to orient growth as desired. Branches can be moved gradually over several months. Thin back vigorous, upright sprouts.

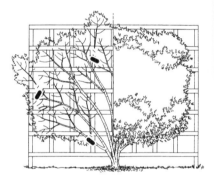

After: Shear back protruding sprouts to 2 to 4 sets of leaves, and continue to remove vigorous upright stems.

Common camellia

BOTANICAL NAME: *Camellia japonica*

PLANT TYPE: Evergreen Ornamental Informal Espalier Shrub

SIZE: Unpruned plants grow 6'–12' tall and wide.

GROWING HABITS: Slow to moderate growth rate. Well-branched evergreen with very ornamental glossy dark

green leaves and many colors of bloom. Grows well in large containers that can be moved to a more protected place for the winter. Prefers partial shade; good for shady entryways and eastern- and northern-facing patios. Terminal-flowering shoots make their bloom in spring.

Common camellia *(continued)*

TIME TO PRUNE: Pruning to enhance bloom should be done after blooming or in midsummer. Prune in summer to whatever shape you have in mind.

NEW SHOOTS AFTER CUTTING BARE STEMS? Will form shoots from old growth.

SPECIAL PRUNING POINTERS: Pick or clip out flowers with camellia petal blight (brown in the center of the blossom) and destroy.

STEP BY STEP: *1.* Choose a plant with a strong central leader and leave it uncut after planting—it can be headed back once it has reached the top of your trellis. *2.* Tie new shoots to the trellis as soon as they are long enough. Head back certain shoots to dormant buds to form more laterals. *3.* Allow some side branches to remain uncut. Then the tip bud will grow vertically and make length. During the summer, tie the vertical portion of the shoot down to the angle you want to fill in the form. *4.* In midsummer in cold-weather climates and up to fall in moderate-winter areas, cut back much of the new growth to just above the point where last year's growth terminated—look for the scar of wrinkles that denote the change in years. Use hand clippers. This pruning will stim-ulate three or more shoots and flower buds for next spring.

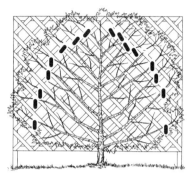

Before: In spring, tie lateral branches to the trellis and head them back to encourage branching.

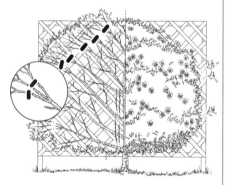

After: In summer, cut back new growth to near its origin.

Oriental or Chinese or Japanese persimmon

BOTANICAL NAME: *Diospyros kaki*

PLANT TYPE: Deciduous Fruit Tree Informal Espalier

SIZE: Unpruned trees grow to 30'. Can be kept considerably lower with summer pruning, perhaps down to 6'–8'.

GROWING HABITS: Slow-growing tree with leathery, dark green oval leaves. It usually exhibits fantastic fall color.

The fruit left on the tree after leaf fall act as winter ornaments. As a free-standing tree, seldom needs pruning except for occasional shaping and the usual removal of damaged, diseased, or dead tissue. This is a terminal-flower-ing (bearing) plant. Fruit appears near the ends of current year's growth. (Uneven watering will cause the fruit to fall off the tree.)

Oriental or Chinese or Japanese persimmon *(continued)*

TIME TO PRUNE: Most often pruned in summer to control growth and shape the canopy.

NEW SHOOTS AFTER CUTTING BARE STEMS? Will make some growth, but not as prolific or reliable as most trees.

SPECIAL PRUNING POINTERS: Nothing special; a very well-mannered tree.

STEP BY STEP: *1.* Buy a tree with branches close to the graft. Or, purchase a whip (maiden) and cut to 6"–12" above the graft to bring about a number of shoots that will become the primary scaffold. (If the bare-root tree is branched, you can still cut down to 6"–12" above the graft.) Tie to the trellis as soon as possible. Train the tree into a random pattern or an informal fanlike shape. Remember, the branches will show each winter. *2.* Summer pruning is used to remove unwanted growth and to control the tree's height as it reaches the top of your trellis. Tie shoots to the trellis where the canopy is thin or missing. *3.* During the winter, clip some branches to existing dormant buds to invigorate more branching where the canopy needs to be filled in.

Apple, European pear

BOTANICAL NAMES: *Malus pumila, Pyrus communis*

PLANT TYPE: Deciduous Fruit Tree Formal Espalier

SIZE: On the proper dwarfing rootstock, can be kept to 4'–8" tall and 6'–15' wide. Be sure to get a dwarfing rootstock that will help control the tree to the height of your trellis.

GROWING HABITS: Reasonably fast-growing spur-type trees. Apple spur systems can bear fruit for up to 20 years and pears have productive spur systems for 5 or more years.

TIME TO PRUNE: Spring pruning is useful for stimulating new growth in the form of laterals and shoots. Summer pruning is used to control unwanted growth, reduce vigorous growth, and stimulate shoots into flower buds (and eventually spurs).

NEW SHOOTS AFTER CUTTING BARE STEMS? Produces new shoots with abandon.

SPECIAL PRUNING POINTERS: Both trees are somewhat susceptible to fire blight, but the pear is more sensitive. The usual remedies apply: Cut all damaged branches 12"–18" past the visible damage into clean, green growth. Be sure to clean your shear's blades *after each cut* with a 10% bleach-and-water solution, 100% Lysol™, or 100% rubbing alcohol.

STEP BY STEP: The pruning procedures for apple and pear trees are very similar; one variety can be more vigorous than the other, depending on the dwarfing rootstocks used. The more vigorous trees require heavier spring and summer pruning to control their height, or a bigger wall or trellis. The steps for each form of espalier are different, but the principles are the same. Two forms will be described here, ones which use the natural dynamics of the tree to form fruit: the Belgian arch (arcure method) and the oblique cordon.

TO GROW A BELGIAN ARCH (ARCURE METHOD): This is the easiest form to grow for both structure and fruit. The Belgian arch relies on the simple

Apple, European pear *(continued)*

dynamics of the tree's food and hormones after the gardener bends a branch into an arch. *1.* Purchase only whips (maidens) that are 3'–4' tall. Plant each whip at a slight angle facing either the left or right side of the trellis. Plant 3'–5' apart depending upon which dwarfing rootstock is being used. Leave the tip buds uncut. *2.* Allow the whips to grow unencumbered. Clip back (head) or pinch all side shoots (laterals) once they grow 12" or more, then remove 4"–6". (This is the beginning of summer pruning to turn laterals into flower spurs.) *3.* By midsummer, bend the whips over to form the arches. (If you can find 5'- to 6'-tall whips, they can be arched immediately after planting.) Secure each arched whip in two places to the trellis, halfway up each side of the arch. Allow some of the dormant buds along the top portion of each arch to sprout into vertical shoots. *4.* As soon as it's apparent which new vertical shoots are the most vigorous, head back all other vertical shoots to turn them into flowering spurs. On

each arch, leave one healthy, new vertical shoot to become the next arch. *5.* During the summer, continue to head back or pinch all laterals progressively a little farther back each time. Do this two, three, or four times. In late summer, head each lateral back to three true leaves with their buds. By now, the former dormant buds at the base of each leaf stem should have fattened to show the characteristic swollen, rotund shape of next spring's flower bud. *6.* Late in the summer, bend each vertical shoot over to form another arch. Bend them in the opposite direction from the lower course of arches. Tie the arched shoots onto the trellis in two places if possible. *7.* Each year, form an arch on each tree to the opposite direction so the arches curve symmetrically up the trellis. At the top of the trellis, use summer and spring pruning to control the height by thinning out all vertical shoots along the tops of the upper arches. Continue to progressively head back all lower shoots to promote flower buds and their subsequent spur systems.

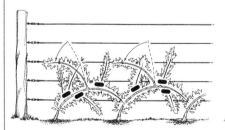

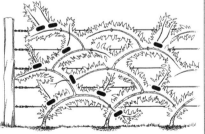

Before: In summer, arch spring-planted fruit trees over and secure them to the trellis. Later, a vigorous upright lateral will become an arch that grows in the opposite direction.

After: Repeat for several years until the arch system fills up the trellis. Continue to remove any unnecessary upright-growing shoots, and pinch back side branches into spurs.

Apple, European pear *(continued)*

TO GROW AN OBLIQUE CORDON: This is the second-easiest method for espaliering. Not well known, but far easier to espalier for the novice. *1.* Buy only bare-root maidens. Plant the *entire* tree at a 45° angle with the bud union of the graft on top. (This method produces the same results as training a fruit-tree limb to the ideal 45° angle—equal production of vegetative shoots and flower buds.) Try growing more than one. Plant them 2'–4' apart, depending upon how strongly the rootstock dwarfs the plant, or for reasons of style. *2.* Tie a 4'–6', 1" × 1" stake at a 45° angle. Align the stake at the tip of the angled whip and tie it securely to the trellis. This will be used to train what was the central leader of the whip to a 45° angle. *3.* After the tip bud of the leader grows 1' or more, tie the new shoot to the stake with green garden tape. Continue this process of bending down and tying the leader all summer. *4.* Prune all new shoots (laterals) for flower formation throughout the summer with repeated pinching or heading cuts to control all lateral growth. Two, three, or four times a summer, clip the lateral a little farther back than the pre-

vious time. The last cut should remove all but three mature leaves with fat flower buds at the base of each stem. *5.* There is a simpler, less time-consuming way to form fruit, but it doesn't keep the crown as architecturally manicured as the classic pattern. When each lateral gets 8" or more long, weight it down with one or more clothespins. This forms an arch like a miniature Belgian arch and causes heavy flowering on the outside of the arch next spring. Thereafter, the weight of the fruit continues to hold the limb in a fruitful arch and the clothespins are moved to new shoots. This makes for somewhat jumbled growth. The "flat" portion of the tree may be 4' or more deep instead of less than 2' deep with a classic oblique cordon. But the overall effort is considerably reduced compared to typical summer pinching and clipping. This is sort of an Americanized form of the classic ideal. *6.* When the trees reach the top of the trellis, use summer and spring pruning to control the height with thinning cuts. Use spring pruning only to remove unwanted shoots that were obscured by foliage during the summer.

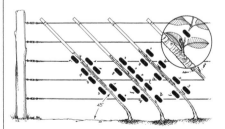

Before: Plant young trees at a 45° angle and secure them to a trellis. Tie the leader to a stake that will maintain the 45° orientation.

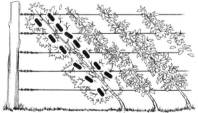

After: To maintain a mature oblique cordon, thin back upright shoots and pinch back lateral branches to spurs that will bear fruit.

INDEX

(Page numbers in *italics* refer to illustrations.)